wire art

jewelry

WORKSHOP

wire art jewelry

WORKSHOP

Step-by-Step
Techniques and Projects

SHARILYN MILLER

www.sharilynmiller.com

INTERWEAVE.
interweave.com

Editor Rebecca Campbell
Designer Lee Calderon
Photographer Joe Coca
Photo Stylist Ann Swanson
Step-by-Step Photographer Sharilyn Miller
Production Katherine Jackson
Video Studio Manager Garrett Evans
Video Producer Rachel Link
Video Content Producer Rebecca Campbell

Interweave Press LLC
201 East Fourth Street
Loveland, CO 80537
interweave.com

Printed in China by Asia Pacific Offset Ltd.

Library of Congress Cataloging-in-Publication Data

Miller, Sharilyn.
  Wire art jewelry workshop + DVD : step-by-step techniques and projects /
[Sharilyn Miller].
      p. cm.
   Rev. ed. of: Wire art jewelry. c2009.
   Includes bibliographical references and index.
   ISBN 978-1-59668-408-9 (pbk. + DVD)
   1. Jewelry making. 2. Wire craft. 3. Beadwork. I. Miller, Sharilyn. Wire art
jewelry. II. Title. III. Title: Wire art jewelry workshop plus DVD.
   TT860.M563 2011
   745.594'2--dc22

                                2010029893

10 9 8 7 6 5 4 3 2

acknowledgments

As we wrap up the final details of bringing this book to life, I have several very talented and dedicated professionals to thank. Editor Rebecca Campbell did such a terrific job going over the text, cutting here and there, and asking for additional information where it was most needed. And yes, there was a bit of hand-holding as well! She also oversaw the filming of the DVD that accompanies this book, answered my innumerable questions, and is the one most responsible for pulling together all the details of this hefty project. Book designer Lee Calderon made magic with my text and step-by-step photos, with the help of production designer Kerry Jackson. Thank you, everyone, for making it all look so good! Special thanks also goes out to stylist Ann Swanson and photographer Joe Coca, who took all the beauty shots of my finished jewelry for the cover and chapter intro pages. I'm always taken aback when I see my jewelry lit perfectly and photographed in a setting designed by a professional. Finally, I want to make special mention of Garrett Evans, video studio manager, and producer Rachel Link, who worked with Rebecca Campbell to produce the supplementary DVD. It's a joy to work with professional creatives who really know what they're doing. Thank you for making me feel more at ease in front of your video cameras! You know that I could not have produced *Wire Art Jewelry Workshop* (book and DVD) without you. I deeply appreciate all the creative talent, effort, and many hours of work that you invested in this endeavor.

Sharilyn

I *love* working with wire to make art jewelry. Perhaps the main reason comes down to the wire itself: It's soft enough to manipulate easily, but strong enough to hold a permanent shape once it's been hammered and worked with tools. It's the ideal sculpting and building medium because it can be cut to any length and then shaped, bent, twisted, spiraled, looped, and coiled into whatever design your heart desires.

Wire inspires me. When I take a piece of heavy-gauge wire into my hands, I immediately begin to not only *see* but also *feel* a new design taking shape. To me, this is magical. Perhaps I picture a sinuous bangle wrapped and coiled with finer-gauge wire (see my Double-Spiral Bangle) or maybe the underlying structure for a pendant such as the centerpiece for the Grateful Heart Necklace. As an art material, wire seems to have unlimited potential for jewelry designers.

By working with fine-gauge wire (28-gauge through 22-gauge), you can make intricate little sculptures to dangle from your ears (see the Gypsy Stick and Squiggle Earrings). Moving through the midsize gauges (20-gauge through 16-gauge) allows you to create wire links and bead wraps appropriate for numerous bracelets, anklets, necklaces, and chokers. My personal penchant is for heavy-gauge wire—14-gauge through 10-gauge—because it is more challenging to work with.

Wire is available in different tempers: dead-soft, half-hard, and full-hard. I tend to purchase mine in a dead-soft condition and trust that it will work-harden enough through manipulation with my hands and tools. I shop catalogs and online sources for the best prices on silver wire, but I also find copper wire in various gauges at my local hardware store. Sometimes I'll use yellow brass wire or the newly popular dark annealed steel wire (hardware store finds, again), but my personal preference is for sterling silver or fine silver. My theory is that, since I put a lot of time and effort into my jewelry, I'd like the end result to have some intrinsic as well as artistic value.

The type of wire you work with comes down to personal choice. You'll find finished projects in this book made with both sterling silver and copper round wire. I always recommend purchasing at least some copper wire to experiment with before committing to working with the more expensive silver wire. If you're creating a brand-new design and trying to determine correct measurements, use copper wire to work out the kinks in your design. There will be some waste, but the cost is minimal when working with copper.

Another great way to make the most of your trials and errors is to keep a small notebook on your worktable. I use a notebook to take careful notes of wire gauges and measurements as I'm working out new designs. Trust me, you won't remember this information later. It's very helpful to write everything down as you work. Later, when you want to make a valuable jewelry piece using silver or gold wire, you'll be glad to have written directions for every link, bead wrap, and jump ring.

Another thing to know about wire is that it comes in many shapes as well as diameters, measured in gauges. For instance, you can find round wire, square wire, half-round wire, triangle wire, even bead-wire (this is not really wire but silver beads soldered together). Every artist eventually develops a personal preference for one or two wire types; my favorite is round. Occasionally I will use half-round wire for coiling, and I have used heavy bead-wire to make big jump rings. All of the projects in this book and on the accompanying DVD are made with round wire.

Wire Art Jewelry Workshop also includes an instructional DVD featuring close-up instruction on some of the techniques found in the book. For instance, you can watch as I twist fine-gauge wire in a drill and then use the twisted wire to form tapered "worm beads" on a pointed mandrel. If you have trouble with knotless netting or double-coiling fine-gauge wire, watch these segments on the DVD and all will become clear to you. Additional chapters cover heavy-gauge wire used to make beautiful jump-ring rosettes, figure-eight links, and more.

I hope that you enjoy learning some new techniques from this book and DVD and that the projects I've presented within these pages will stimulate your own creativity. Don't be afraid to make changes to the designs you see here—that's what being a creative artist is all about. You can do this, and I encourage you to try.

Happy wrapping!

tools & materials

You will need some fine-quality tools for making wire art jewelry, and I recommend purchasing the best that you can afford. They will give you a lifetime of jewelry-making pleasure. Inexpensive tools can be frustrating to work with, especially for beginners. Although they might seem to be economical, inexpensive tools will have to be replaced. Fortunately, wire artists need only purchase a handful of tools to get started in this rewarding art form. Besides tools, you will need to purchase a few supplies such as wire, beads, and miscellaneous items.

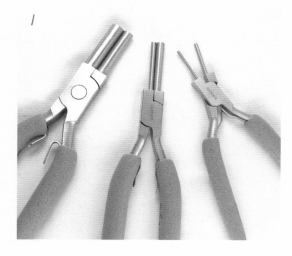

pliers

Bail-forming pliers are not essential, but I really appreciate having them in my toolbox. I tend to use the largest size pliers *(pictured 1)*, but it is helpful to know that they come in different sizes. They're quite useful for making wire coils and jump rings and for forming large loops for wire links and ear wires.

Not an essential tool—you can do without it—but a pair of **bent chain-nose pliers** *(pictured 2)* are very helpful when opening and closing jump rings.

Chain-nose pliers *(pictured 3)* are an absolutely essential tool on the jeweler's workbench. Look for a tool with a smooth tapered jaw, a flat surface, and a joint that opens and closes easily. Avoid cheap pliers from the hardware store with serrated surfaces; they'll mar your wire or sheet metal and cause you endless headaches.

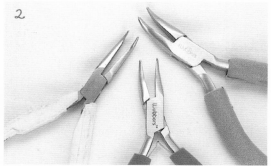

wire art jewelry workshop

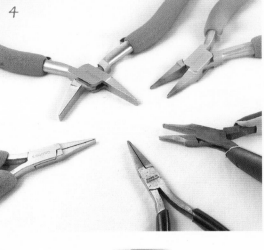

Flat-nose pliers *(pictured 4)* are very similar to chain-nose pliers with their flat inner jaws and straight sides, but, instead of tapering to a point, they have a straight edge. These pliers come in various widths and different lengths as well as handle types. You need only one pair to start with, and I suggest searching for a pair with comfortable handles. *Tip:* I like to remove the springs on my pliers or bend them back, but this is a personal choice.

Another essential tool, **round-nose pliers** *(pictured 5)*, is best purchased in two sizes. Small round-nose pliers are used to start small spirals and for creating tiny loops and shapes in wire. Larger round-nose pliers are used to make big loops and ear wires. Look for a good-quality pair with comfortable handles.

cutters

A very good-quality pair (or two) of **flush cutters** is essential for wirework. I use my heavy-duty pair *(pictured 6, left)* for 18-gauge to 12-gauge wire and my finer pair *(pictured 6, right)* for delicate wire in gauges from 20-gauge to 28-gauge. It's very important not to use your finer tool on heavy wire because within a short time you can easily ruin the tool. *Tip:* When cutting wire heavier than 10-gauge, it's best to use a jeweler's saw.

tools & materials

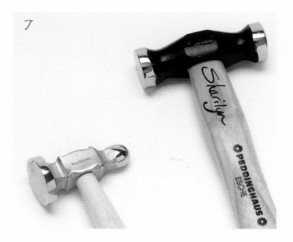

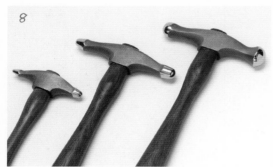

Chasing and planishing hammers *(pictured 7)* are used on a bench block, bracelet mandrel, and other surfaces to forge or flatten wire and sheet metal. Look for a good-quality hammer with a slightly rounded (convex) face. A chasing hammer with a flat face is not useful for wirework because you can't get a smooth transition between the round and flattened wire unless the surface of the hammer's face is rounded in a convex curve. Many chasing hammers on the market have perfectly flat faces, so examine your hammer carefully before purchasing it.

Texturing hammers *(pictured 8)* are very useful for creating marks in flattened wire and sheet metal. These marks create a dimpled or weathered look, adding character to an otherwise smooth jewelry component. Experiment with different hammers to create varied effects.

Hard plastic (resin) and rawhide mallets *(pictured 9)* are used to shape wire without flattening or marring it. Rawhide mallets may be used in place of plastic, but they must be conditioned first by hammering them against a hard surface to soften the edges. Using plastic or rawhide mallets work-hardens the metal.

Steel bench blocks *(pictured 10)* are used as a base for hammering jump rings, clasps, and wire links. They're also used when shaping and texturing wire with various hammers. The two sizes shown here are 2½" x 2½" (6 x 6 cm) and 4" x 4" (10 x 10 cm). The smaller bench block is quite versatile and useful for many applications and has the added advantage of being easy to pack for traveling wire artists. The larger block comes in handy when working big wire shapes as well as sheet-metal pieces. Look for a good-quality bench block made of case-hardened tool steel with a flat, polished surface.

mandrels

Bracelet mandrels and a vice *(pictured 11)* are very useful for shaping and hammering metal—wire, tubing, or sheet—

in a particular shape and size in order to make bracelets and bangles. They come in a smooth tapered style or with "stepped" sizes *(pictured)*. Note that bracelet mandrels can also be used to hammer and shape wire for a variety of other purposes, such as making large hoop earrings or rounded wire links with huge curves. *Tip:* When using a bracelet mandrel, it's helpful to place it in a vice attached firmly to your workbench.

Easily found in most hardware stores and jewelry supply catalogs, a **center punch** *(pictured 12)* is used in this book as a mandrel or tool for wrapping wire in a tapered coil. The coil is then used to make "worm beads" (see the Basic Techniques section) for bracelets and necklaces.

general tools

An accurate **tape measure** and **6" (15 cm) ruler** are invaluable tools that you will use every day while making wire jewelry.

Jewelry files *(pictured 13)* are available in many sizes, shapes, and qualities. Your toolbox should include a few small needle files (flat, round, half-round, and triangular) as well as some larger files. I like having a couple of larger files (flat and half-round), purchased from a jewelry catalog, plus a few inexpensive large files purchased from hardware stores. I use my cheap files first to begin rough-filing a piece, then switch to jewelry-quality files, and finish by polishing the metal with steel wool. Some jewelry artists also like to use sandpapers in various grits before polishing with steel wool. *Tip:* A natural wine cork makes a terrific handle for these types of files (not shown in photo).

You'll need a **drill** *(pictured 14)* for twisting fine- and heavy-gauge wire. I twist 16-gauge wire to make twisted-wire jump rings and finer-gauge wire (such as 26-gauge and 24-gauge) for wrapping and coiling techniques. Look for a good-quality powerful drill with a keyless chuck that can be easily opened and closed with your fingers.

11

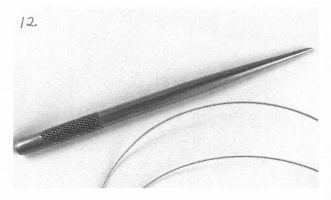
12

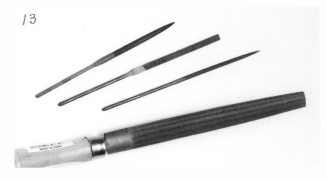
13

14

tools & materials

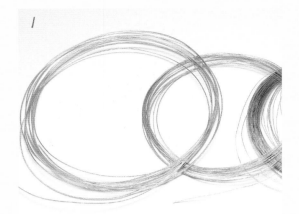

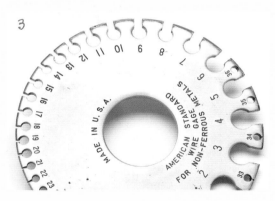

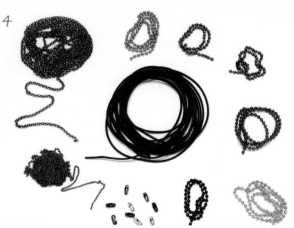

wire

Sterling silver and copper round dead-soft wire *(pictured 1 and 2)* was used in all of the projects in this book. Wire can be purchased from suppliers in large rounds or on spools, in various diameters from 28-gauge to 10-gauge (and even heavier). Copper wire also can be found in hardware stores, but be sure to purchase round dead-soft wire for the projects featured in this book.

A **wire-gauge measuring tool** *(pictured 3)* like this one is used for measuring wire, tubing, and sheet metal. To use it, press the metal (sheet, tubing, or wire) against the slots until you find one that offers some resistance. If it goes in too easily, the metal is smaller or finer than the gauge number indicated on the slot. Note that the holes at the end of each slot are not used for measuring the metal but for easily drawing it out of the tool.

0000 (superfine) **steel wool** is used to clean wire and sheet metal prior to using it. Steel wool is also used for polishing metal surfaces after applying chemical agents to them (such as liver of sulfur). You can find steel wool in various grades at any hardware store; look for superfine steel wool, indicated by the four zeros highlighted on the package.

beading supplies

Necklace-making materials *(pictured 4)* can include copper chain, silver ball-chain, rubber lacing, sterling silver neck wires, leather strips, ribbons, fibers, satin cording, braided threads, etc. If you like the industrial look, chains made from inexpensive metals such as copper or colored metals are a terrific alternative to traditional precious-metal chains. Most bead stores carry a variety of copper and brass chains as well as fine sterling silver chains and neck wires.

Beads *(pictured 5)* are available in such a wide variety of shapes, sizes, colors, textures, and materials that it would be impossible to show you all of the possibilities here. I always encourage my students to experiment and try beads and pearls of different sizes and shapes, which is why I rarely specify a particular size or shape when teaching my workshops. In general, I look for beads with large holes, gemstones that are well-cut and faceted, and lampworked beads that have been annealed properly in a kiln to avoid breakage. I always seek the best-quality pearls that I can afford; it makes a difference. I avoid using cheap plastic beads, but have had great success with quality resin beads as well as some beads made of various types of hardwood.

Washers *(pictured 6)* are found in some hardware stores and specialty stores such as Harbor Freight. They come in different diameters and can be altered quite easily with texturing hammers, files, and rolling mills. Use them in place of jump rings in bracelet and necklace designs for an ethnic look.

Head pins *(pictured 7)* can be handmade from copper, gold-filled or sterling silver wire, or purchased commercially. While I often make my own head pins, I also enjoy using handmade Bali silver head pins that are so ornate and delicate, I could never make them myself. Use head pins to create bead dangles for earrings, bracelets, and necklaces.

Liver of sulfur *(pictured 8)* is used to artificially age metal—particularly copper and silver, although it also works on yellow brass—and it is more economical to buy it in chip form, as shown. The chips come in a metal airtight container with a tightly sealed lid. It's always best to store your liver of sulfur in a cool, dry place and keep the lid on at all times. Never store liver of sulfur in direct sunlight or near moisture as it will quickly degrade.

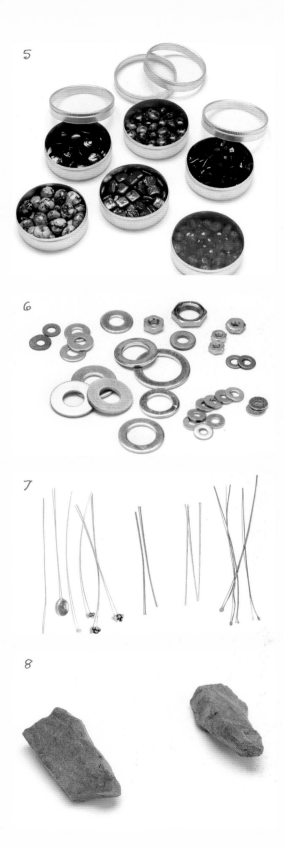

5

6

7

8

tools & materials

basic techniques

Bead Connectors
WITH DOUBLE-WRAPPED EYE-PIN LOOPS

Bead connectors made with double-wrapped eye-pin loops are useful in most bracelet and necklace designs. Practice making a few of them with inexpensive beads and copper wire until you feel confident of your abilities. Then you can switch to silver or gold wire to make components for finished jewelry. Also try making small double-wrapped eye-pin loops using fine wire for earrings and dainty bracelets and then switch to heavier gauges of wire for big necklaces and bold, chunky bracelets.

materials

- Bead of your choice
- Round dead-soft wire in your choice of gauge (about 6" [15 cm]); note that this measurement will vary depending on the length of bead used

tools

- Ruler
- Flush cutters
- 0000 (superfine) steel wool
- Jewelry pliers: small round-nose, chain-nose, and flat-nose

  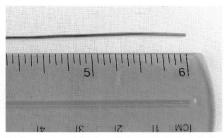

1 Choose a bead and then test various gauges of wire on it until you find the correct gauge for the bead. Clean the wire thoroughly with 0000 (superfine) steel wool.

2 Flush-cut one end of the wire.

3 Measure and flush-cut about 6" (15 cm) of wire (this measurement varies, depending on the length of the bead you're using).

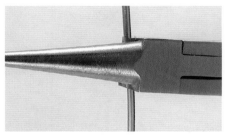 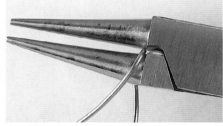 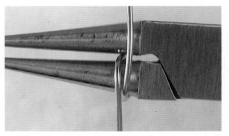

4 Take hold of the wire in the back of the small round-nose pliers, about one-third of the way from the top of the wire.

5 Roll your hand around, taking the wire around the bottom jaw of the round-nose pliers.

6 Continue rotating the tool in your hand until the wire has been carried around the tool once and is now flat across both jaws of the tool.

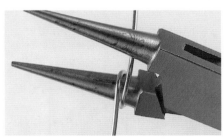 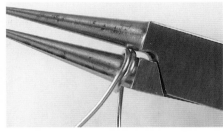 

7 Open the pliers and bring the top jaw on top of the wire in preparation for creating a second loop.

8 Rotate the tool around in your hand as in Step 5.

9 Continue rotating the tool in your hand until the wire has been carried around the tool a second time and is now flat across both jaws of the tool.

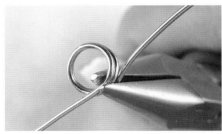  

10 Remove the round-nose pliers. Grasp the wire in the tips of the chain-nose pliers as shown.

11 Bend the wire sharply back against the edge of the tool. This is known as "breaking the neck."

12 Remove the chain-nose pliers. Reinsert the round-nose pliers as shown, with the wrapping wire on the bottom of the two loops.

bead connectors with double-wrapped eye-pin loops

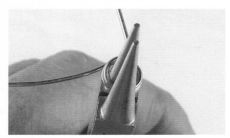

13 Place the tool in your left hand, with the wrapping wire to the left and the longer wire facing directly away from you.

14 Grasp the wrapping wire end in the tips of the chain-nose pliers and wrap it over quickly to the right.

15 Wrap the wire under, to the left.

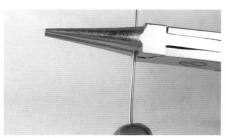

16 Remove the round-nose pliers. Turn the wire over so that you can grasp it about ½" (1.3 cm) above the bead, in the back of the round-nose pliers.

17 Roll your hand around, taking the wire to the right of the bead, around the bottom jaw of the round-nose pliers.

18 Continue rotating the tool in your hand, rolling the wire onto the pliers. Stop when the wire has been carried around the tool a second time and is now flat across both jaws of the tool.

19 Remove the round-nose pliers. Grasp the wire in the tips of the chain-nose pliers as shown. Bend the wire sharply back against the edge of the tool.

20 Remove the chain-nose pliers. Reinsert the round-nose pliers. Place the tool in your left hand, with the wrapping wire to the left and the bead facing directly away from you.

21 Grasp the wrapping wire end in the tips of the chain-nose pliers and wrap it over quickly to the right.

22 Wrap the wire under, to the left.

23 Continue wrapping each wire around the "neck" area between the eye-pin loop and the bead. Trim any excess wire with flush cutters and press the wire ends down firmly with the chain-nose pliers. As an alternative, spiral in the wire using chain-nose pliers.

wire art jewelry workshop

Bead Dangles
WITH DOUBLE-WRAPPED EYE-PIN LOOPS

Double-wrapped eye-pin loops add a touch of elegance to bead dangles that can be used in various jewelry designs, from earrings to necklaces and charm bracelets. Practice making several before attempting to make a finished piece of jewelry; your goal is perfect round eye-pin loops of equal size and a tightly wrapped "neck" beneath the loops. With this technique, practice makes perfect.

materials

- Bead or pearl of your choice
- Head pin of your choice (commercial or handmade)

tools

- Flush cutters
- Jewelry pliers: small round-nose and chain-nose

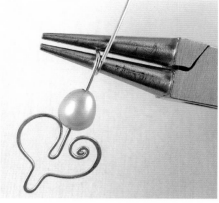

1 Place a bead or pearl on the head pin of your choice—this can be a commercial head pin or one that you've made following the instructions in this book. Take hold of the wire in the middle of the small round-nose pliers, about ½"–¾" (1.3–2 cm) above the bead.

2 Bend the wire around the bottom jaw of the pliers.

3 Continue bending the wire around the tool until you have made one complete rotation, with the wire lying flat across the tool. Pressing your left thumb against the wire against the tool as you turn it will help to form a tight round loop.

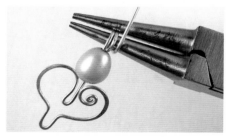

4 To start the second loop, first open up the tool wide to get the top jaw of the pliers out of the way.

5 Close the tool and wrap the wire around the bottom jaw again, wrapping the second loop closely adjacent to the first one.

6 To create a complete double loop, the wire must lie flat across the tool as shown. It may look like three loops, but if you turn the tool over, you will see that you actually have two complete loops.

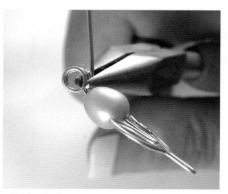

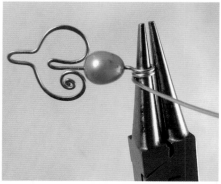

7 Remove the round-nose pliers and insert the tips of the chain-nose pliers into the double loops, right next to the bead.

8 Press the bead straight back, carrying the wire with it, so that the wire is bent firmly against the edge of the chain-nose pliers. This action is known as "breaking the neck."

9 Remove the chain-nose pliers and reinsert the round-nose pliers with the long wrapping wire on the bottom as shown.

wire art jewelry workshop

10 Place the tool in your left hand, with the long wrapping wire to the left and the bead on its head pin facing directly away from you.

11 Use chain-nose pliers to pull the wire sharply up and over to the right. Pull the wire under to begin wrapping the "neck," which is the area between the eye-pin loop and the bead.

12 Wrap over and under this neck area, from the double eye-pin loop down toward the bead, as many times as you desire.

13 *Option:* Trim the wire end if necessary using fine-quality flush cutters.

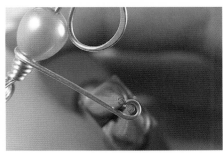

14 *Option:* To create a small spiral with the remaining straight wire, bend a tiny loop in the wire end using the tips of the round-nose pliers.

15 Tighten down the tiny loop in the tips of chain-nose (or flat-nose) pliers.

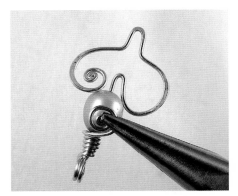

16 Spiral in the wire tightly or loosely (as shown) until you reach the bead and then press the spiral gently against the bead. Your bead dangle is now ready to use in a pair of earrings or in a necklace or bracelet design.

cleaning wire

Wire is rarely clean right out of the package. It's often marred by surface oxidation, dirt, and sometimes even sticky residue from tape. For this reason, always clean wire thoroughly before using it to make jewelry. I use 0000 (superfine) steel wool from the hardware store to clean my wire. A large package costs around $4 to $5 and should last several months. Tear off a hunk and roll it into a tight ball and then wrap the steel wool around the wire. Pull the wire through the steel wool, squeezing the wool firmly with your fingers as you do so. You may have to repeat this action a few times to remove stubborn dirt. This process cleans and simultaneously straightens and polishes wire. It also warms it and work-hardens the metal slightly. If you start with dead-soft wire, which I recommend, the small amount of work hardening caused by cleaning it should not be cause for concern. As an alternative to using steel wool, try using jewelry polishing pads or cloths. Whatever product you use, be sure to clean your wire before using it to make jewelry. It's much easier to clean straight wire than to try cleaning a finished wire link or coil-wrapped bead, which may have tiny crevices where dirt can hide.

Bead Dangles
WITH SINGLE-WRAPPED EYE-PIN LOOPS

Making bead dangles for earrings, bracelets, and necklaces is an essential skill that you'll have to master very early on if you're going to make jewelry with wire. Fortunately, it's not difficult to learn if you follow the steps provided here and practice them until your eye-pin loops are perfectly round and centered.

materials

- Bead or pearl of your choice
- Head pin that will fit through your bead or pearl

tools

- Flush cutters
- Jewelry pliers: small round-nose, chain-nose, flat-nose

1 Place a bead or pearl on the head pin of your choice and grasp the head pin about 1" (2.5 cm) above the bead with small round-nose pliers.

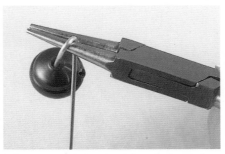

2 Press your left thumb against the head pin, against the tool, and turn your right wrist up, carrying the wire around the lower jaw of the round-nose pliers.

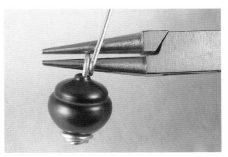

3 Continue turning the tool until the wire has been shaped around it as shown. Note that the wire end was carried to the right, toward the box-joint on the tool. Also note that the size of the eye-pin loop will be determined by your placement of the wire on the tool.

4 Remove the round-nose pliers and insert the tips of the chain-nose pliers into the loop, near the bead. Bend the loop back against the edge of the tool. This is known as "breaking the neck."

5 Remove the chain-nose pliers and reinsert the round-nose pliers. Place the tool in your left hand in preparation for wrapping the "neck" area between the eye-pin loop and the bead. Note that the wrapping wire is situated beneath the loop, not on top of it.

6 Holding the round-nose pliers in your left hand, grasp the wrapping wire end with chain-nose pliers and bring the wire up and over across the neck.

7 Pull the wire around and under the first wrap.

8 To finish, you can trim the wire end with flush cutters or create a tiny "baby spiral" on the wire end to add a decorative touch. Start the spiral in the tips of small round-nose pliers.

9 If necessary, tighten the beginning spiral using either flat-nose pliers (shown) or chain-nose pliers.

10 Use flat-nose pliers to spiral in the wire toward the bead. Continue spiraling in the wire until you reach the bead and then tilt the tool slightly to press the spiral against the bead.

11 Use flat-nose pliers to gently squeeze the wrapped eye-pin loop to flatten it. *Option:* Use flat files to file away any tool marks or burrs in the wire. Round files may be used to file away marks in the eye-pin loop.

bead dangles with single-wrapped eye-pin loops

Cage Beads

Cage beads are versatile elements that add a bit of whimsy to bracelets and necklaces. I think they're fun and easy to make. Best of all, cage beads can be changed easily by using various gauges and wire types (silver, gold, brass, copper). For example, for a bold, earthy look, try using 14-gauge copper wire, or for a more delicate jewelry piece, make your cage beads with 18-gauge sterling silver or gold-filled wire.

materials

• Round dead-soft wire: 10" (25.5 cm) 16-gauge

tools

• Flush cutters
• Hard-plastic mallet
• Ruler, tape measure
• Small steel bench block
• 0000 (superfine) steel wool
• Chasing hammer with a convex face
• Jewelry pliers: small round-nose, chain-nose, and flat-nose

1 Clean the wire thoroughly with 0000 (superfine) steel wool.

2 Place the wire in the small round-nose pliers, about ¼" (6 mm) from the tips of the tool.

3 Bend a half-loop in the wire.

4 Quickly twist your wrist to wrap the wire around the beginning spiral. Repeat Steps 2–4 with the opposite end of the wire, but spiral in the opposite direction (see Step 6 for an illustration).

5 Switch to chain-nose pliers and spiral in the wire some more, on both ends.

6 Continue spiraling in each wire end equally. Stop when the two spirals meet in the middle.

7 If the wire is a bit crooked or misshapen, hammer it flat with a hard-plastic mallet.

8 To remove tool marks, lightly flatten the double spiral with a chasing hammer. Don't overdo this! Very light forging with the chasing hammer should remove most or all of the tool marks.

9 Poke the tips of round-nose pliers through the center of a spiral. Repeat with the other spiral. Both spirals should point in the same direction.

10 Switch to flat-nose pliers and grasp the wire in the precise middle. Bend the wire over in one swift motion.

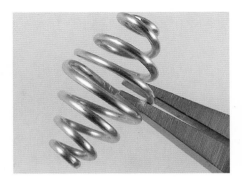

11 Use the flat-nose pliers to tweak the cage, straightening out any unwanted bumps in the wire and separating the wires equally for a beautifully shaped bead.

12 Set the cage aside and flush-cut a 2" (5 cm) piece of 16-gauge wire. Bend a loop in the wire in the middle of the small round-nose pliers.

cage beads

13 Switch to chain-nose pliers. Grasp the wire inside the loop, right where the wire end touches itself.

14 Bend the wire straight back against the edge of the tool.

15 Reinsert the round-nose pliers and straighten out the wire so that it resembles a lollipop.

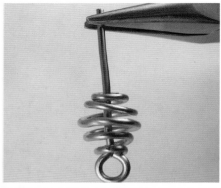

16 Run the straight wire through one end of the cage.

17 Bend the wire over in the middle of the round-nose pliers.

18 "Break the neck" as before, using chain-nose pliers and switch to round-nose pliers to straighten the loop on the wire.

cage beads

Cage beads are easy and fun to make in a variety of sizes and different wire gauges. They look great whether you fashion them from copper wire as shown or from sterling or fine silver, gold-filled, or even brass wire. Try making big cage beads using 10" (25 cm) to 12" (31 cm) of 14-gauge wire or much smaller beads using 6" (15 cm) to 7" (18 cm) of 20-gauge wire—or even finer wire if using the cage to capture very small pearls. Also try using twisted wire to make cages. Twist about 2' (.6 m) of 20-gauge wire (this results in slightly less than 1' of finished twisted wire) and follow the instructions on the previous pages to make a cage bead from it. Also try twisting 1' (.3 m) of copper and 1' (.3 m) of silver wire together for a mixed-metals look.

Celtic Knot
LINKS

Celtic knot links may seem mysterious, but they're really nothing more than interlocking coils of wire held together firmly with simple eye-pin links. Using large bail-forming pliers helps to make each link the same size and shape. Try making your Celtic knot links in different sizes and in varying wire gauges for your own distinctive look.

materials

- Round dead-soft wire in 16-gauge (about 4' [122 cm]) and 14-gauge (about 1' [30 cm])

tools

- Flush cutters
- Ruler, tape measure
- 0000 (superfine) steel wool
- Jewelry pliers: small round-nose, bail-forming, chain-nose, flat-nose

1 Clean your wire thoroughly with 0000 (superfine) steel wool. Flush-cut some 16-gauge wire about 4' (122 cm) long to make several Celtic knot links.

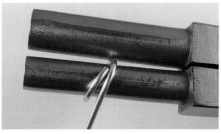

2 Place one end of the 16-gauge wire in the jaws of large bail-forming pliers and begin forming a coil on the smaller (6.8 mm) jaw. As you turn the pliers over in your right hand, bring the long end of the wire to the right of the cut end. Continue coiling.

3 You're aiming for a long coil of equally sized links, each coil adjacent to the one preceding it, with no gaps between coils. Continue coiling.

4 When you've run out of wire to coil, press down the last ¼" (6 mm) of wire using flat-nose or chain-nose pliers.

5 Remove the coil from the pliers and flush-cut one end using fine-quality flush cutters.

6 Insert chain-nose pliers into the coil and count six links. At this point, grasp the coil firmly and tilt the tool back, separating coil six from coil seven.

7 Flush-cut the coil, allowing some overlap between the cut ends so that on the top it appears that you've cut a six-link coil. If you turn the coil over, you'll see that it's really a five-link coil.

8 From this angle, count the coils again. It looks like six coils, but this is due to the ¼" (6 mm) overlap between the coil's cut ends. Use chain-nose pliers to reshape the coil, if necessary, and set it aside. Flush-cut the long coil (from Steps 2–6) and repeat Steps 7–9. Continue cutting off short coils until you run out of wire.

9 Pick up two short coils and insert one end of one coil into the center of the other coil.

10 Use your fingers or chain-nose pliers to turn the coil around and around, like a key ring, until the coils are interlinked.

11 A finished interlinked coil pair looks like this. Note that the wire ends on each coil have been "buried" inside the link so that they don't show. It may be necessary to trim the wire ends on one or both coils in order to hide them, but take care not to cut them too short, or the links won't lock together securely.

12 Flush-cut about 2" (5 cm) of 14-gauge wire and form a small eye-pin loop on one end as shown, using the small round-nose pliers.

13 "Break the neck" using chain-nose pliers.

14 Reinsert the round-nose pliers into the eye-pin loop and center it on the straight wire.

15 Insert the straight wire end into an interlocked coil pair from Steps 9–11.

16 Push the wire through the coils diagonally so that it emerges on the opposite side as shown. This secures the link.

17 Create a second eye-pin loop. If the wire is a bit too long, just trim it with a flush cut and reshape the loop.

18 The finished Celtic knot with a simple eye-pin link is now ready to use in a necklace or bracelet design.

Coil-Wrapped
BEAD CONNECTORS

The "recipe" provided in this section results in coil-wrapped wire that is quite versatile and will fit a wide variety of beads in different sizes and shapes. If you wish to coil-wrap wire for very tiny beads or pearls, try using very fine wire such as 24-gauge or even 26-gauge. For very large, chunky beads or pendants, try using heavier wire gauges to make a coil-wrapped embellishment.

materials

• Round dead-soft wire: 18" (45.5 cm)
  20-gauge, 6" (15 cm) 18-gauge

tools

• Flush cutters
• Ruler, tape measure
• 0000 (superfine) steel wool
• Jewelry pliers: large round-nose,
  chain-nose, flat-nose

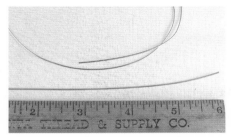

1 Clean your wire thoroughly with 0000 (superfine) steel wool. Measure and flush-cut 6" (15 cm) of 18-gauge wire and 18" (45.5 cm) of 20-gauge wire. Bend the 20-gauge wire in half.

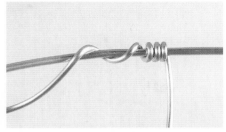

2 Wrap the 20-gauge wire tightly around the 18-gauge base wire.

3 Continue wrapping tightly.

4 When you've wrapped as much wire as possible on one end, press it firmly against the base wire using chain-nose pliers.

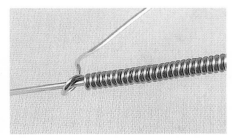

5 Pull the coiled wire to the opposite end of the base wire.

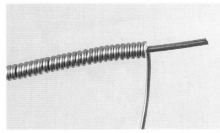

6 Wrap the 20-gauge wire around the base wire.

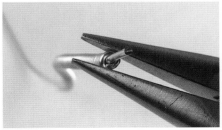

7 When you've wrapped as much wire as possible, press it down firmly.

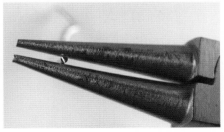

8 Insert one end of the base wire into the jaws of large round-nose pliers, about one-fourth of the way from the tips of the jaws.

9 Turn the tool over to wrap the wire around it, wrapping toward the box-joint on the tool.

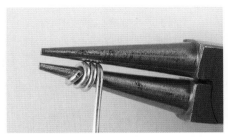

10 Wrap three times and stop.

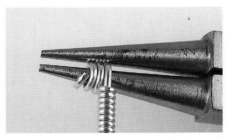

11 Push the coil up to the tool, turning the end of the coil inward so that it cannot be seen.

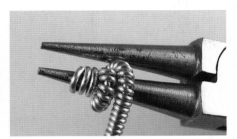

12 Continue wrapping the wire around the tool.

coil-wrapped bead connectors

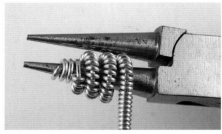

13 As you wrap the coiled wire around the tool, a bead begins to form.

14 Shift the bead toward the tips of the pliers and continue to bend it into a bead shape.

15 Stop when you run out of coiled wire. Notice that the bead is shaped with tapered ends.

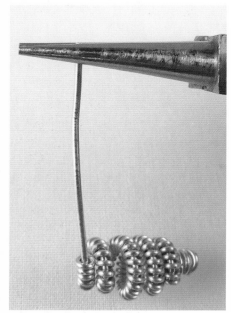

16 Grasp the base wire end in the round-nose pliers, about one-fourth of the way from the tips of the jaws. Notice that the bead is facing to the right. Wrap the wire around the lower jaw of the pliers by turning the tool away from you.

17 When you reach the coiled wire, stop.

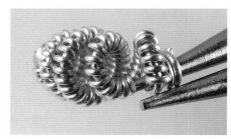

18 Remove the round-nose pliers, turn them around, and reinsert them into the coiled wire from the opposite end.

19 Hold onto the bead and twist the tool until the bead is shaped correctly.

20 To insert a bead, first twist the coiled wire open with your fingers.

coiled-wire beads

Another option is to make your own beads by simply using coiled wire. Follow Steps 1–19 until you have a finished, tightly coiled wire bead as shown in the photo from Step 19. Set it aside. Skip Steps 20–21; you won't need a separate bead for this technique. Next, cut a piece of 16-gauge wire about 2" (5 cm) long and form a simple (unwrapped) eye-pin loop on one end as shown in Steps 23–25. Insert the straight end of the wire into the coiled-wire bead and trim the 16-gauge wire end until about ¾" (2 cm) of wire protrudes from the coiled-wire bead. Form another simple eye-pin loop with this wire. You now have a coiled-wire bead connector, which can be used in both necklaces and bracelets.

21 Place a bead of your choice inside the coil-wrapped wire. Tighten the coil-wrapped wire if necessary to fit the bead closely.

22 Insert wire into the bead, running it through one end of the coil-wrapped wire, then through the bead, and out the opposite end of the coil-wrapped wire. *Tip:* Always use the heaviest gauge wire that will fit through your bead. In the sample shown, about 6" (15 cm) of 16-gauge wire was used.

23 Place one end of the 16-gauge wire in the middle of the small round-nose pliers. Roll your hand over, turning your palm up, to bend the wire around the tool until it touches itself.

24 Use chain-nose pliers to bend a sharp angle in the wire. This is known as "breaking the neck."

25 Reinsert the small round-nose pliers and bend the loop forward, centering it on the straight wire. The first eye-pin loop is finished.

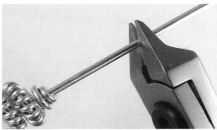

26 Push the coil-wrapped wire and bead against the first eye-pin loop. Measure about ¾" (2 cm) away from the opposite end of the coil-wrapped wire and flush-cut the wire with wire cutters.

27 Grasp the wire end with small round-nose pliers as in Step 25 and bend the wire forward to form a loop.

28 If there is a "neck" area of straight wire between the coiled wire and the end of the loop, trim some of the wire back using flush cutters.

29 Reinsert the round-nose pliers and re-form the loop.

30 "Break the neck" with chain-nose pliers as in Step 24.

31 Reinsert the small round-nose pliers and bend the loop forward, centering it on the straight wire. The first eye-pin loop is finished.

32 Use chain-nose pliers to press down the coiled wire ends if needed.

coil-wrapped bead connectors

Free-Form Knotless
NETTING

Free-form knotless netting is a fun way to add a creative wire embellishment to medium- and large-size beads, such as the type used to make pendants. Any shape or color bead may be used for this technique, but the best beads are somewhat flat, with plenty of design area on which to embellish. Depending on the wire gauge you use and the size of your bead, you may need more or less wire than I used in the sample.

materials

- One large pendant bead
- Round dead-soft wire in a fine gauge such as 24, 22, or 20 (about 4' [122 cm])

tools

- Flush cutters
- Tape measure
- 0000 (superfine) steel wool
- Jewelry pliers: small round-nose, chain-nose, flat-nose

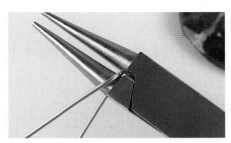

1 Clean the wire with 0000 (superfine) steel wool. Flush-cut 4' (122 cm) of wire (20-gauge was used in the sample) and bend it in half with the small round-nose pliers.

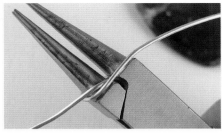

2 Continue to bend the wire around in a loop at the back of the tool.

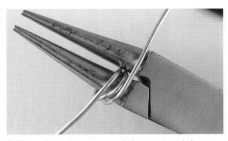

3 Wrap the wire a second time around the tool.

4 Use round-nose (or chain-nose) pliers to bend back the straight wire. This is how a double eye-pin loop is formed.

5 Place the round-nose pliers in your left hand and wrap the straight wire up and over to the right. This is called "wrapping the neck."

6 Wrap a second time, very tightly.

7 Place a large pendant-size bead on the wire that has been wrapped.

8 Grasp the wire about 1" (2.5 cm) away from the end of the bead in the round-nose pliers.

9 Wrap the wire down toward the bead, twice around the tool, as in Steps 2–3.

10 Wrap the neck. Working on one end of the bead, wrap a large loop of wire around in a circle. This is known as "casting a line." Hold down the large loop.

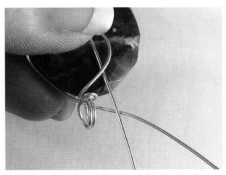

11 Bring the wire end up and then point it down into the large loop. Pull it through.

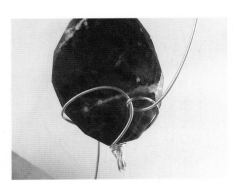

12 Pull the wire firmly until you have created a small overhand knot tied to the large loop from Step 11.

free-form knotless netting

13 Tie another overhand knot below the first one.

14 Continue tying knots on the first large loop.

15 Start working with the wrapping wire from the opposite end of the bead, casting a line as in Step 10.

16 Once you've created one large loop on the bead, bring the wire up and then down through one of the knots created in Step 14.

17 Continue tying knots in this manner, on both sides of the bead, tying knots to knots in a free-form manner that looks pleasing to you.

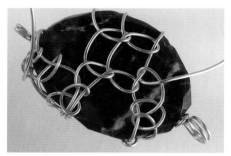

18 Almost done: The secret to free-form knotless netting is knowing when to stop. Too much is definitely too much, and it shows.

19 It may be necessary to flush-cut some excess wire on one or both ends of the bead.

20 Begin to spiral in the wire ends, starting with the tips of the small round-nose pliers.

21 Spiral in the wire with either flat-nose or chain-nose pliers. Tuck the spiral against the bead and repeat Steps 13–18 with the wire on the opposite end of the bead.

knotless netting

Knotless netting is a great way to embellish plain beads, especially large, flat pendant-size stones. But it tends to obscure a bead's surface, so it's not the best choice for embellishing fancy beads with lots of surface detail.

French Ear
HOOKS

Once you know how to make beautiful handmade head pins and bead dangles with wrapped eye-pin loops, finish the look with a pair of handmade French-style ear hooks. By making these ear hooks with a wrapped loop, you'll ensure that the bead dangles never separate from the hooks. Personalize yours with a fancy spiral for a decorative touch.

materials

- Two bead dangles for each pair of earrings
- Round dead-soft wire: 6" (15 cm) of 20-gauge or 22-gauge

tools

- Ruler
- Flush cutters
- Small steel bench block
- 0000 (superfine) steel wool
- Chasing hammer with a convex face
- Jewelry pliers: large round-nose, small round-nose, and chain-nose

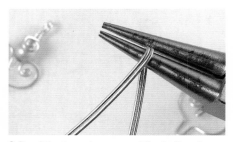

1 Start with two finished bead dangles on your choice of head pin (commercial or handmade) and about 6" (15 cm) of round dead-soft wire flush-cut into two 3" (7.5 cm) long pieces. Clean the wire with 0000 (superfine) steel wool.

2 Whenever I make a pair of ear hooks, I always start them together to ensure they look the same. Line up the two wire pieces and insert them side by side in the middle of the small round-nose pliers, with one-third of the wire above the tool as shown.

3 Bend the two wires around the bottom jaw of the round-nose pliers. Pressing your left thumb firmly against the wire as you bend it around the tool will help to form round, tight loops.

4 Bend the wires until they're wrapped all the way around the tool.

5 Remove the round-nose pliers and insert the tips of the chain-nose pliers into the loops.

6 Bend the two wires back firmly against the edge of the chain-nose pliers.

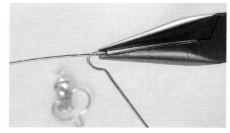

7 Remove the chain-nose pliers from the loops. Separate the two wires and begin working with them one at a time. Insert the small round-nose pliers into one wire loop. Bend the loop forward just slightly until it's centered perfectly on the long straight wire.

8 Remove the small round-nose pliers. Open the loop sideways using chain-nose (or flat-nose) pliers.

9 Place a bead dangle on the loop and close the loop firmly.

10 Reinsert the small round-nose pliers into the loop, with the wrapping wire beneath the loop. Turn the tool straight up and place it in your left hand with the longest wire facing directly away from you and the shorter wrapping wire facing left.

11 Grasp the wrapping wire in the tips of the chain-nose pliers and wrap the wire over the loop.

12 Continue wrapping under and over a few times.

wire art jewelry workshop

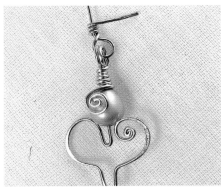

13 Quit wrapping when you have about three wraps and ½" (1.3 cm) of straight wire remaining.

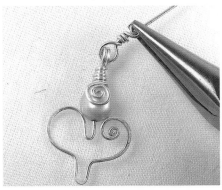

14 Spiral in the short wire using chain-nose pliers until it's centered on the longer straight wire as shown.

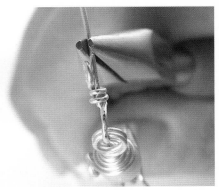

15 Grasp the long straight wire just a tiny bit above the spiral in chain-nose (or flat-nose) pliers.

16 Bend the wire over the spiral.

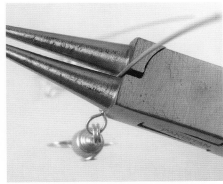

17 Place the wire in the back of large round-nose pliers right up against (but not inside) the box-joint on the tool. The wire should be pointing toward you.

18 Use your fingers to bend the wire firmly around the tool, forming an ear hook–shape.

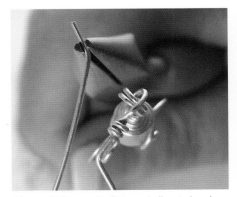

19 Use chain-nose (or flat-nose) pliers to bend up the last ¼" (6 mm) of wire, which makes it easier to run the ear hook into your pierced earlobe. *Option:* File the wire end with a flat file or use a cup-burr on a small handheld drill to smooth the wire end. This is especially important if you cut your wire with inexpensive cutters, which often leave burrs on the wire.

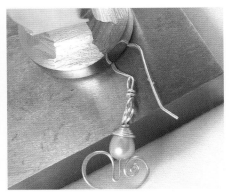

20 *Option:* Hammer the rounded portion of the ear hook on a small steel bench block, using a chasing hammer with a slightly convex face. Take care to hammer the wire lightly, as you don't want to thin down the wire too much.

Heart-Shaped
HEAD PINS

Handmade heart-shaped head pins are different, aren't they? Thankfully, they're not too difficult to make—although they do require a few more steps than other types of head pins. Like other head pins, however, when you make your own you have control over how long your head pins will be, what type of metal they'll be made from, and the wire gauge, too.

materials

- Round dead-soft wire in your choice of gauge (about 6" [15 cm] for each head pin)

tools

- Ruler
- Flush cutters
- Small steel bench block
- 0000 (superfine) steel wool
- Chasing hammer with a convex face
- Jewelry pliers: large round-nose, small round-nose, chain-nose, and flat-nose

1 Clean the wire thoroughly with 0000 (superfine) steel wool or a polishing cloth. The wire used in the sample is 22-gauge round dead-soft sterling silver.

2 Flush-cut one end of the wire, taking care to cover the wire with your finger to keep the cut end from flying away and hitting someone.

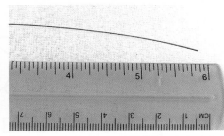

3 Measure and cut about 6" (15 cm) of wire for each head pin.

4 Create a tiny loop on one wire end using the tips of the small round-nose pliers.

5 If necessary, close the loop down tight using the tips of chain-nose (or flat-nose) pliers. Begin spiraling around the loop; this can be done in the tips of the chain-nose pliers as shown or with flat-nose pliers.

6 As you spiral the wire, allow the spiral to open up a bit. A loose, open spiral with a tight center is what we're aiming for.

7 Use flat-nose pliers to bend a sharp angle in the wire as shown.

8 Shift the flat-nose pliers to a new position.

9 Use your thumb to bend the wire up and around the edge of the flat-nose pliers.

10 Shift the position of the flat-nose pliers and bend the wire sharply against the edge of the tool.

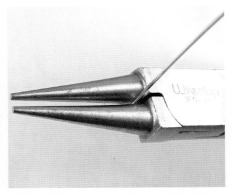

11 Switching to large round-nose pliers, place the wire in the back of the tool next to (but not inside) the box-joint on the tool.

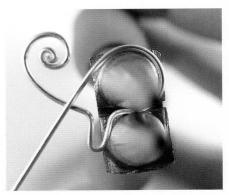

12 Turn the round-nose pliers so that the tips face you and you can look down the tool while you wrap the wire up and around the top jaw. This forms the second "hump" in the heart shape.

heart-shaped head pins

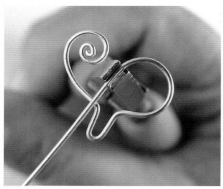

13 Switch to small flat-nose pliers again and grasp the wire in the position shown.

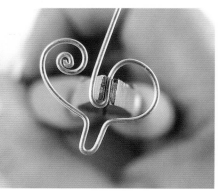

14 Bend the wire around and up, using the tool to shape the wire.

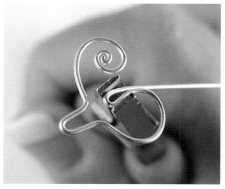

15 Gently press the two wires so that they lie close to one another.

16 Use a chasing hammer to forge the outer edges of the heart shape, taking care to avoid other areas of the heart.

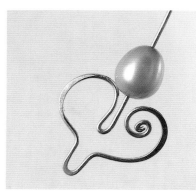

17 The finished heart-shaped head pin is ready to use with the bead or pearl of your choice.

fancy head pins

Heart-shaped head pins are just one of many options the creative jewelry designer has when it comes to personalizing her pieces. Try these techniques as well:

• Use a kitchen torch to "ball up" wire ends to make head pins in different lengths and wire gauges. This technique works well with fine silver, sterling silver, and even copper wire.

• Create a large open spiral on one wire end, hammer it flat, and texture it with an embossing hammer. Try making spirals in different sizes and pairing them with beads in various sizes and shapes. A big, bold spiral head pin might look just great with a tiny pearl; you'll never know unless you try it!

• Try shaping copper wire in various shapes, such as triangles, squares, or rectangles or organic forms such as flowers, stars, and leaves. Place these wire shapes on your worktable and then place a bead or pearl above each one. When you find a shape that you like, use sterling silver wire to make a head pin utilizing this shape. Place a bead on it, wrap an eye-pin loop above the bead with the straight wire, and you have a charming bead dangle with your own original touch.

Hook-and-Eye
CLASP

This hook-and-eye clasp is useful for any jewelry design in which the artist does not wish to draw attention to the clasp. It is so simple and basic, it "disappears" into the overall composition, much like a jump ring. But, like a jump ring, even the simplest clasp should be well made, with attention to craftsmanship.

materials

- Round dead-soft 14-gauge wire: 4½"
  (11.5 cm) (copper, brass, gold, or silver)

tools

- Ruler
- Flush cutters
- Small steel bench block
- 0000 (superfine) steel wool
- Chasing hammer with a convex face
- Jewelry pliers: large round-nose, small round-nose, bail-forming, and chain-nose

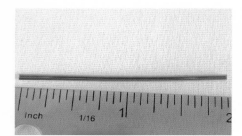

1 Clean the wire with 0000 (superfine) steel wool and measure and flush-cut a 2" (5 cm) piece.

2 Place the wire in the large bail-forming pliers.

3 Bend the wire up and around the largest (8.8 mm) jaw on the bail-forming pliers, turning the tool until the wire touches itself.

4 Remove the tool and insert chain-nose pliers into the loop right where the wire touches. Bend the wire sharply back against the edge of the tool. Reinsert the bail-forming pliers to reshape the wire as in any other eye-pin loop.

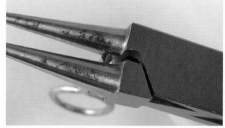

5 Place the straight wire end in the back of the small round-nose pliers, against (but not inside) the box-joint. Make sure that the large eye-pin loop made in Steps 2–4 is oriented so that you can look through it.

6 Bend the wire up, over, and around the round-nose pliers, as in Step 3, turning the tool until the wire touches itself.

7 Remove the round-nose pliers and bend the wire back with chain-nose pliers.

8 Reinsert the round-nose pliers and bend the loop forward until it's centered perfectly on the other larger loop.

9 The finished "eye" of the hook-and-eye clasp.

10 Measure and flush-cut a 2½" (6.5 cm) piece of 14-gauge wire. Hammer the end with a chasing hammer on a bench block to thin down the wire, making it easier to bend.

11 Bend a tiny loop in the hammered end of the wire, in the tips of the small round-nose pliers.

12 Use chain-nose pliers to close the loop if necessary.

wire art jewelry workshop

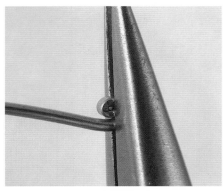

13 Spiral-in the wire just a bit, using chain-nose pliers.

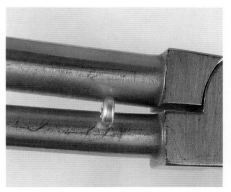

14 Place the wire, spiral facing you, in the bail-forming pliers. Orient the pliers so that the largest (8.8 mm) jaw is farthest from you.

15 Bend the wire up and over until it touches itself, forming a hook shape.

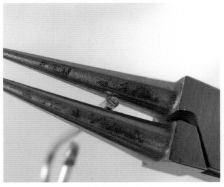

16 Place the straight wire end in the middle of the small round-nose pliers.

17 Bend the wire up and over until it touches itself, forming a loop.

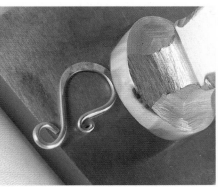

18 Hammer the back of the hook shape to flare it out a bit (don't overdo this step), and the hook is finished. File it if necessary to remove any tool marks.

hook-and-eye clasp

The hook-and-eye clasp demonstrated on these pages is a good place to start; the clasp is functional and looks fine with most bracelet and necklace designs. But you can easily make simple changes to the design to vary the look, depending on the type of jewelry you make.

Consider using very heavy gauges of wire—such as 14- or even 12-gauge—to make a chunky clasp for a big, bold necklace. Use a little bit more wire (experiment first with inexpensive copper), hammer it more as needed, and try using a small embossing hammer to texture the flattened wire from Step 18.

You can also try making a smaller hook-and-eye clasp using 18-gauge wire instead of the recommended 16-gauge that I used in the previous pages. Don't use wire in a finer gauge than that, however, because it won't be sturdy enough to hold a jewelry piece together securely. Always keep in mind that your jewelry should be functional and well made, as well as beautiful.

Jump Rings

Making your own jump rings is a valuable, basic skill that will save you money and provide more creative control over your jewelry designs. By making them yourself, you choose the type of wire (round, square, half-round, etc.), metal (copper, silver, gold), the wire gauge, and the size and shape of your jump rings. The only way to really ensure quality control is to make your own jewelry components by hand. Fortunately, it's easy!

materials

- Round dead-soft wire in your choice of gauge (about 2'–3' feet [61–91.5 cm])

tools

- Flush cutters
- Ruler, tape measure
- 0000 (superfine) steel wool
- Jewelry pliers: large round-nose, small round-nose, bail-forming, chain-nose, bent chain-nose, flat-nose

1 Cut a generous length (2'–3' [61–91.5 cm]) of wire in the gauge of your choice. The wire shown in the sample is 2' (61 cm) of 14-gauge round dead-soft sterling silver. Clean your wire thoroughly with 0000 (superfine) steel wool.

2 Flush-cut one wire end.

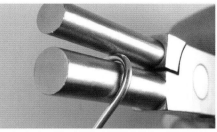

3 Place the flush-cut end of the wire in the round-nose-type jewelry pliers of your choice. Consider using small round-nose, large round-nose, or bail-forming pliers; the tool you use will help determine the size jump rings you make. For the sample, I used the large (8.6 mm) jaw on my favorite pair of bail-forming pliers.

4 Begin coiling the wire onto the tool, pressing your thumb against the wire against the tool to help shape it.

5 Continue rolling the length of wire onto the tool until a long coil emerges. The coil will consist of equally sized rings.

6 When you get to the end of the wire, it will be work-hardened. You'll have to introduce a pair of flat-nose or chain-nose pliers to press the wire end down firmly. This finishes the coil.

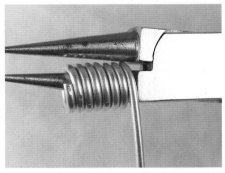

7 Here's another coil of wire, shaped this time on the back of the large round-nose pliers. The diameter of this coil is smaller than the coil made on the bail-forming pliers. Experiment with this technique, making lots of jump rings of different sizes on different pliers or other shaping tools such as knitting needles.

jump rings

I love making my own jump rings by hand, as demonstrated on these pages. But if you need to make hundreds of rings for chain-mail or other jewelry designs, consider investing in a mechanical jump-ring maker of some type (different brands are available). You will need a flex-shaft to cut the rings unless you use a jeweler's saw instead. Using a saw is more time-consuming. Depending on your experience level, you might find that you can hand-cut jump rings with flush cutters faster than sawing them apart. But the advantage to using a saw is that each ring is cut perfectly flush on both ends, and there is very little waste. This is especially important to consider if you are making your jump rings from costly metals such as gold or silver. Always save your precious metal for recycling—powder from sawing or tiny cut-off bits from cutting wire. Keep these bits in separate containers; for example, all sterling silver cutoffs and powder from sawing should be kept in its own container separate from fine silver or other metals. Once you have a collection of metal bits, you can turn it in for recycling and receive cash or credit in return.

8 Remove the pliers and flush-cut one end of the coil.

9 Turn the flush cutters over in your hand. Using the cut end of the wire to guide your cutters into the coil, grip the wire and bend it back a little so that you can more easily cut the wire in the middle of the tool rather than the tip.

10 Turn the flush cutters over in your hand. Flush-cut the wire end as shown and then repeat Steps 7–9 until you've used up the entire coil of wire.

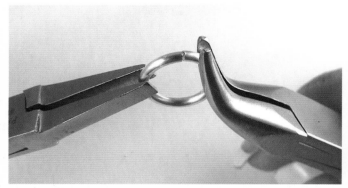

11 It's necessary to "condition" your jump rings by wiggling the ends back and forth until they click together. Examine them closely and press the wire ends down if they don't meet perfectly.

12 Use a hard-plastic or rawhide mallet to hammer and work-harden your jump rings. This adds the finishing touch that will set your jump rings apart from the work of amateurs. Once you have a collection of conditioned jump rings in various sizes, store them in labeled containers for future use.

Rosette Jump-Ring
CLUSTERS

Clusters of three intertwined jump rings resemble a rosette pattern that will add a unique touch to bracelet and necklace designs. If you use large jump rings in heavy-gauge wire, the clusters take the place of a more complicated wire link.

A fun option might be to make jump rings from three different colored metals such as silver, gold-filled, and copper or silver, yellow brass, and copper. Combine your jump rings as demonstrated on these pages for a lovely mixed-metals look.

materials

- Jump rings in your choice of gauge and metal, three rings per cluster

tools

- Jewelry pliers: bent chain-nose, flat-nose

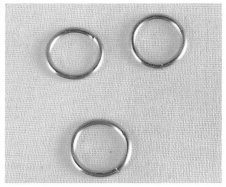  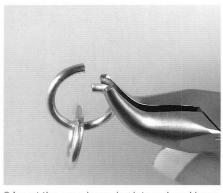

1 Start with three large jump rings made on the 8.6 mm size jaw of large bail-forming pliers. Make sure the rings have been conditioned properly and closed securely (see the chapter on making jump rings for details).

2 Open one jump ring sideways using bent chain-nose and flat-nose pliers or two pairs of flat-nose pliers if you have them.

3 Insert the open jump ring into a closed jump ring.

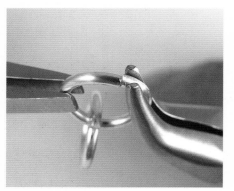  

4 Close the jump ring securely. This is easy to do if the ring was conditioned properly beforehand.

5 Two intertwined jump rings.

6 Open the third jump ring sideways and insert it into the center of the two intertwined jump rings from the previous step.

7 Close the third jump ring securely. Set aside the rosette cluster, make several more, and you're ready to assemble a bracelet or necklace.

Simple (unwrapped)
EYE-PIN LOOP BEAD CONNECTORS

This is an easy way to make perfectly round unwrapped eye-pin loops every time, using round-nose and chain-nose pliers. This is a basic technique that every jewelry artist should master. Here's how to make perfectly round loops, nicely centered on the bead, without much or any "neck" area between the bead and the loops.

materials

- Bead
- Round dead-soft wire in the gauge of your choice (about 3" [8 cm])

tools

- Ruler
- Flush cutters
- 0000 (superfine) steel wool
- Jewelry pliers: round-nose, chain-nose

1 Clean the wire thoroughly with 0000 (superfine) steel wool.

2 Flush-cut one end of the wire you've chosen for your project.

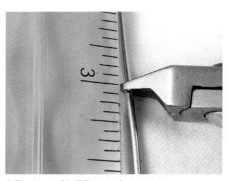

3 Flush-cut 3" (7.5 cm) of wire; this measurement will be important later.

4 Place the wire in round-nose pliers, remembering that the placement in the tool will determine the size of the eye-pin loop. Pull the wire down as far as you can into the tool and use your finger to ensure that you cannot feel the end protruding.

5 Roll the wire around the tool until the wire touches itself.

6 Remove the round-nose pliers and insert the chain-nose pliers into the loop, right where the wire touches itself.

7 Bend the straight wire back against the edge of the tool beneath the loop.

8 Remove the chain-nose pliers and reinsert the round-nose pliers.

9 Rock the loop forward until it's centered on the straight wire.

wire art jewelry workshop

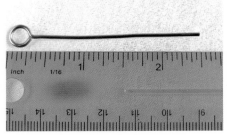

10 Measure the eye-pin loop; the sample shown is 2½" (6.5 cm) long. This means that ½" (1.3 cm) of wire was used to form the loop.

11 Place a bead on the wire.

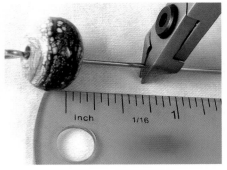

12 Flush-cut the wire, allowing slightly more than ½" (1.3 cm) of wire to make the second eye-pin loop.

13 Repeat Steps 4–6.

14 Repeat Steps 7–8.

15 Repeat Steps 9–10.

simple unwrapped eye-pin loops

Simple (unwrapped) eye-pin loops are usually not as noticeable as other elements such as fancy embellished wire, big textured spirals, shaped wire links and charms, etc. But they should nevertheless be made with care.

If your first attempts are not successful, try practicing by making several eye-pin loops with scrap copper wire. I always encourage my students to practice the same techniques over and over again to improve their craft. Try this: Cut five or six lengths of 16-gauge copper wire, each about 4" (10 cm) long. Next, follow Steps 4–5 with each wire length and set them aside. Then follow Steps 6–7 with each wire length. Finish by following Steps 8–9 with each wire length. By the time you've made several practice eye-pin loops, you will see a noticeable difference in your work.

While I never try to be perfect, I always strive for excellence in my wirework, whether I'm making a complicated embellishment or a simple jump ring or eye-pin loop. Here are some key quality tips:

- Wire ends are always flush-cut—always, no exceptions!

- Make round, shapely loops—no egg or teardrop shapes.

- Close your loops: See how the wire touches itself in the loop from Step 9.

- Remove any tool marks in your wire with careful filing, sanding, and polishing.

Spiral
HEAD PINS

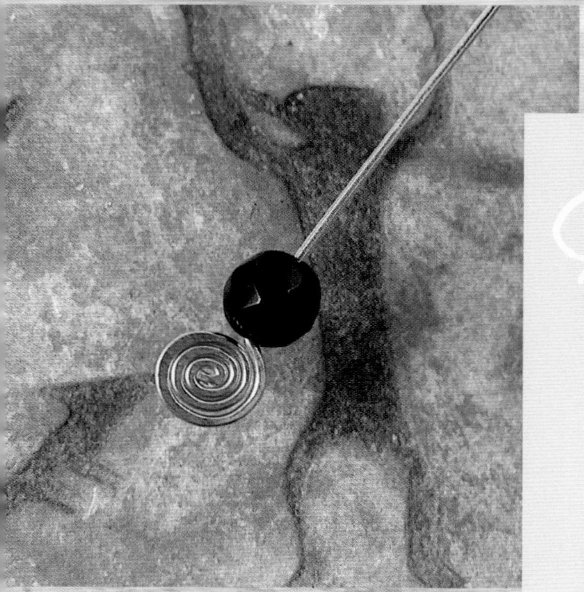

Handmade spiral-shaped head pins are fun and easy to make. Best of all, they're an inexpensive alternative to commercial head pins. When you make your own, you also have more creative control: You decide how long your head pins will be, what metal they'll be made from, and the wire gauge, too. You also control the size, shape, and character of the spiral itself, which has an impact on the finished design.

materials

• Round dead-soft wire in your choice of gauge (about 4" [10 cm] per head pin)

tools

• Ruler
• Flush cutters
• Small steel bench block
• 0000 (superfine) steel wool
• Chasing hammer with a convex face
• Jewelry pliers: small round-nose, chain-nose, and flat-nose

1 Choose some wire in the gauge appropriate for your project and clean it thoroughly with 0000 (superfine) steel wool or polishing cloths.

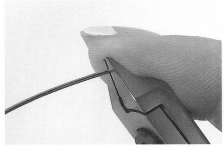

2 Flush-cut one end of the wire, holding your finger over the wire end to keep the little bit from flying out and hitting someone.

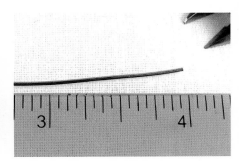

3 Flush-cut the wire to about 4" (10 cm) in length. *Note:* This measurement may vary, depending on your project. The wire used in the sample is 22-gauge round dead-soft copper.

4 Bend a tiny loop on one end of the wire in the tips of the small round-nose pliers.

5 If necessary, close the tiny loop down tight using the tips of the flat-nose pliers.

6 Place the loop sideways in the flat-nose pliers with the loop facing the tip of the tool and bend the wire gently to spiral it.
Tip: The secret to a tight spiral is to bend tiny increments at a time.

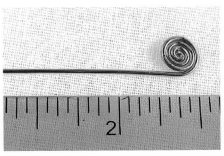

7 Continue spiraling in the wire until it's about 2½" (6.5 cm) long. Again, this measurement may vary, depending on your project.

8 Use flat-nose pliers to bend the wire straight up out of the spiral, resembling a lollipop. If there are tool marks in the wire, don't be concerned. We'll remove those in the next step.

9 *Option:* Hammer the spiral with a chasing hammer, which lightly flattens the wire and removes any tool marks. Place a bead on the straight wire, and you're ready to make a bead dangle for a pair of earrings or a bracelet or necklace.

spiral head pins

Twisting Fine-Gauge WIRE

Use this method to twist fine-gauge (24, 26, 28, etc.) wire for coil-wrapped beads, worm beads, and other techniques. You can also twist two different colors of wire together; my personal favorites are sterling silver and copper wire or sterling silver and yellow brass. Another option when twisting fine gauges of wire is to twist three different colored wires together. It's important, however, that you always twist the same wire gauges together to avoid breakage.

materials

• Round dead-soft wire: 5' (152.5 cm) of 24-gauge, 26-gauge, or 28-gauge

tools

• Flush cutters
• Masking tape
• Tape measure
• Drill with a keyless chuck
• 0000 (superfine) steel wool
• Jewelry pliers: small round-nose

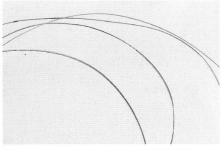

1 Clean your wire thoroughly with 0000 (superfine) steel wool.

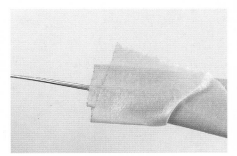

2 Measure and flush-cut about 5' (152.5 cm) of fine-gauge round wire (such as 28-gauge, 26-gauge, 24-gauge).

3 Bend the wire in half and bring the two wire ends together. Wrap them with heavy masking tape or something similar.

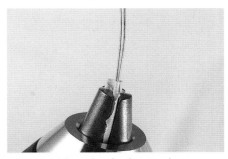

4 Open the keyless chuck on the drill and insert the tape-wrapped wire ends deep into the chuck.

5 Twist to tighten the chuck securely.

6 Take hold of the opposite wire end in the round-nose pliers. Hold the wire straight out from the chuck, turn on the drill, and allow the wire to twist until it breaks at the chuck.

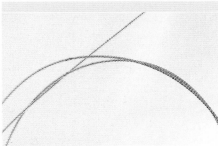

7 The finished twisted wire.

8 Be sure to flush-cut each end. If you started with 5' (152.5 cm) of wire, you should have about 28" (71 cm) of twisted wire. My favorite purpose for fine-gauge twisted wire is to make worm beads. Try using your wire to wrap beads and for other creative purposes.

twisting wire

Consider twisting together two long pieces of 16-gauge or even 14-gauge wire to make decorative jump rings. Once twisted together tightly in a drill as outlined in this chapter, the result will be heavy wire measuring about 11-gauge. With heavier gauges of wire, it is not necessary to tape the ends prior to inserting them into the drill chuck.

Twisted wire can be formed into jump rings of various sizes, snipped with heavy wire cutters or cut with a jeweler's saw, and used in place of plain jump rings in a variety of bracelet and necklace designs. For an alternative look, try twisting sterling silver and copper wire together, or sterling silver and yellow brass or gold-filled wire.

Artificially aging your twisted-wire jump rings in liver of sulfur will accent the metal, giving it form and dimension. Just be sure to twist the same wire gauges together to avoid breakage.

Worm Beads

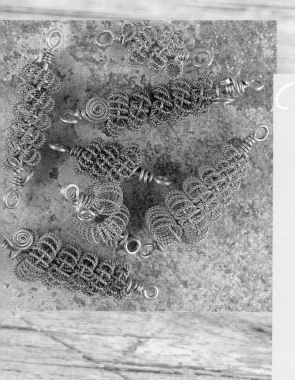

Use twisted fine-gauge wire to make squiggly worm beads—they're fun! They can be made very small for earring dangles or charms, or they can be made quite large for bold necklace components. Turn them into bead connectors by adding either a simple (unwrapped) or wrapped eye-pin loop inside. Your finished "worm" beads can be used in a variety of necklace and bracelet designs.

materials

- Twisted wire: from 5'–10' (152.5–305 cm) for each worm bead
- Round dead-soft wire: about 8" (20.5 cm) 22-gauge, 6" (15 cm) 18-gauge

tools

- Flush cutters
- Center punch
- Tape measure
- Jewelry pliers: small round-nose, flat-nose, and chain-nose

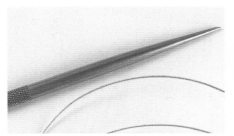

1 Twist several feet of 26-gauge round dead-soft wire (see the chapter on Twisting Wire in the Basic Techniques section). For a small worm bead, twist 5' (152.5 cm); for larger worm beads, twist up to 10' (305 cm). To start a "tapered worm" bead, you'll also need a tapered mandrel such as the steel center punch pictured.

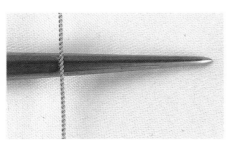

2 Cross the twisted wire over the center punch, near the tip of the tool.

3 Begin wrapping about 2" (5 cm) of twisted wire around the center punch, wrapping toward the tip of the tool.

4 Use flat-nose pliers to gently press down the wire end.

5 Turn the tool over and continue wrapping the twisted wire around it, toward the fatter end of the tool. Wrap as tightly as you can, but know that as soon as you let go of the wrapped wire it will loosen a bit.

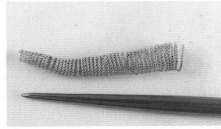

6 Remove the wire from the center punch and set it aside.

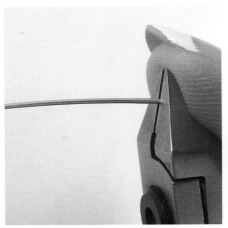

7 Flush-cut about 8" (20.5 cm) of 22-gauge wire.

8 Wrap one end of the wire near the tip of the center punch.

9 Wrap three times and then press the wire down firmly using flat-nose pliers. Place the twisted wire on the 22-gauge wire, small end down.

worm beads

10 Hold down the smallest end of the twisted wire, close to the tool, and pull the 22-gauge wire firmly around the center punch. This may take more than one attempt until you get used to holding the twisted wire firmly as you wrap it from the other end.

11 When you've run out of twisted wire, continue wrapping the 22-gauge wire around the center punch three times. Notice that about half a round of twisted wire is hanging out: this will be trimmed off later.

12 After wrapping the 22-gauge wire three times around the center punch, trim the end with flush cutters.

13 Trim away any excess twisted wire.

14 Use the tips of chain-nose pliers to tighten any gaps in the coiled, twisted wire.

15 Flush-cut about 6" (15 cm) of 18-gauge wire and form a double-wrapped eye-pin loop on one end (see the Basic Techniques section for a chapter on this technique), with a 1" (2.5 cm) tail remaining.

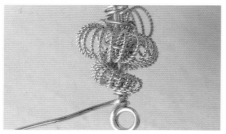

16 Remove the round-nose pliers, turn the eye-pin loop upside down, and place the worm bead on it.

17 Wrap a second double-wrapped eye-pin loop on the opposite end of the wire.

18 Spiral in the little wire "tails," starting with the tips of small round-nose pliers and tightening the beginning spiral with chain-nose pliers if necessary. Spiral in the wire until it meets the bead and then tuck the spiral firmly against the bead.

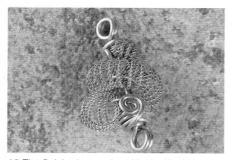

19 The finished worm bead looks like this. It's fairly small because it was made with just 5' (152.5 cm) of 26-gauge wire, which twisted down to 28" (71 cm).

variations

If you wish to make longer worm beads, you will need to use a lot more wire—up to 10' (305 cm), which should twist to about 56" (142 cm).

Another option is to wrap your worm onto 18-gauge wire instead of a center punch, using the wire as a mandrel. This will yield a longer, skinnier worm bead.

Also consider using different wire types for your worm beads, such as plain round or half-round wire.

If you use heavier twisted wire to make your worm beads, such as 22-gauge, you'll need less of it to make a bigger bead.

wire art jewelry workshop

Finishing Techniques
USING LIVER OF SULFUR
AND POLISHING JEWELRY IN A TUMBLER

Using liver of sulfur to blacken silver or copper wire will give your jewelry an antique appearance. Jewelry artists often refer to this as "antiquing," and the technique is an easy way to add a distinctive touch to otherwise shiny-bright metal. It works best with silver or copper wire and is only somewhat effective with yellow brass wire.

materials

- Water
- Plastic fork
- Paper towels
- Glass or ceramic bowl
- Burnishing compound
- Liver of sulfur, dry form

tools

- 0000 (superfine) steel wool
- Mixed stainless-steel jewelry shot
- Jewelry tumbler with rubber barrel

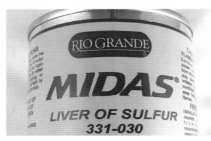

1 Start with a can of liver of sulfur (LOS). My preference is for the dry chips in a small can with an airtight lid. The lid must be pried open with a flat-head screwdriver.

2 Remove a few small chips of LOS and place them in a glass or ceramic bowl. Take care to replace the lid on the can of LOS and hammer it down smartly with a mallet. Meanwhile, heat some water separately.

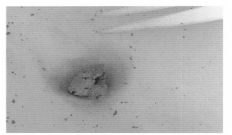

3 Pour the hot (but not boiling) water into the bowl and stir it with a plastic fork to help dissolve the LOS.

4 Place a finished jewelry piece in the bowl of solution while the liquid is still hot and allow the metal to darken.

5 If the solution is very hot, it won't take long for the jewelry to turn completely dark. Take care not to breathe in the vapors; they're not dangerous, just smelly.

6 Remove the jewelry and rinse it in either running water or another bowl filled with clean tepid water.

7 Remove the jewelry from the rinse water and dry it thoroughly with a paper towel.

polishing blackened jewelry

Once the metal in your jewelry has been blackened, it must be cleaned with steel wool and polished by either rubbing it with a jewelry cloth or tumbling it with stainless-steel jewelry shot and burnishing compound. The surface of the metal will become bright and shiny again, but the darkening effect will remain in any areas that your steel wool couldn't reach.

If you neglect to polish the jewelry with steel wool and simply place it straight into the tumbler, even after hours of tumbling the metal will remain black. It will be very shiny, but black! So you must first polish it thoroughly with steel wool.

Allow the jewelry to dry beforehand, making it easier to polish. Also, be sure to leave the blackening effect in all the little crevices of your jewelry piece, which accents wrapped, coiled, textured, and spiraled wire.

Using liver of sulfur to darken metal jewelry will actually emphasize the details, including any tool marks or other defects that have not been polished away beforehand. It's really important to file, sand, buff, and polish your jewelry as much as possible before immersing it in the liver of sulfur solution.

8 Use 0000 (superfine) steel wool to clean the dry jewelry. Rub a round ball of steel wool briskly all over the jewelry to remove the blackening effect of the LOS from the surface of the wire; it remains dark in all the little nooks and crannies. As an option, you may want to scrub the jewelry afterward with some dish soap and a soft bristle brush.

9 To use a tumbler, start with the barrel, which should be stored with the lid tightly secured behind a knob and large washer.

11 Remove the inner liner and fill the barrel halfway full with mixed stainless-steel jewelry shot; about 2–3 lb (.9–1.4 kg) (depending on the size barrel you have). Fill the barrel almost full of water.

10 Remove the knob, the washer, and the outer lid to reveal the inner liner, which has a rubber seal.

12 Place the finished, polished jewelry in the tumbler. Note that if you put jewelry in the tumbler before polishing it with steel wool, the end result is very shiny, clean but black-metal jewelry.

13 Some jewelers use dishwashing liquid to tumble their jewelry, but my preference is to use a product that was designed for the job: Super Sunsheen burnishing compound. Pour a capful of burnishing compound into the barrel and then replace the inner liner, outer lid, washer, and knob (turning it tightly). Place the barrel in the tumbler and turn it on. I usually tumble my jewelry for about 20 minutes, sometimes a little longer. Tumbling times may vary, depending on what types of beads and/or pearls were used in the jewelry. For example, a jewelry piece made with pearls, coral, or turquoise beads should not be tumbled for more than 20 minutes, but an all-metal jewelry piece could be tumbled for hours.

the projects

Gypsy Stick
EARRINGS

Can you just imagine a feisty gypsy woman all dressed up in colorful fabrics and draped in silver chains and bangle bracelets? That's what I think of whenever I make a new pair of my Gypsy Stick earrings. They can be any length and made with a variety of different beads, crystals, pearls, spacers, lengths of coiled wire, found objects—whatever brings out the gypsy in you.

materials

- 2 bead dangles
- 2 French ear wires
- Assortment of small beads
- Round dead-soft wire: 2' (61 cm) 26-gauge, 8" (20.5 cm) 24-gauge, 10" (25.5 cm) 20-gauge

tools

- Flush cutters
- Ruler, tape measure
- 0000 (superfine) steel wool
- Jewelry pliers: small round-nose, chain-nose, and flat-nose

1 Clean your wire thoroughly with 0000 (superfine) steel wool.

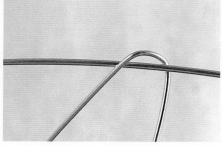

2 Flush-cut 2' (61 cm) of 26-gauge wire and bend it in half over a length of 24-gauge wire.

3 Begin wrapping a tight coil of 26-gauge wire onto the 24-gauge wire.

4 Press down the coil ends very firmly with flat-nose (or chain-nose) pliers.

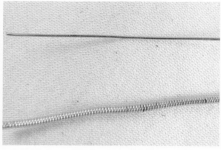

5 Remove the coil from the 24-gauge wire.

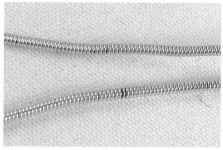

6 Bend the coil precisely in half.

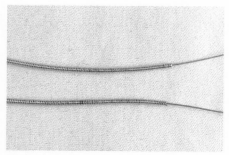

7 Cut the coil at the bend.

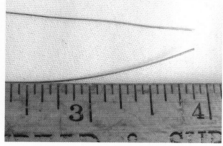

8 Carefully flush-cut the coil ends to remove any sharp burrs.

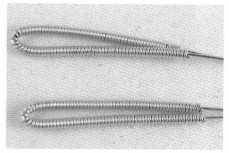

9 Flush-cut two pieces of 24-gauge wire, each 4" (10 cm) long.

10 Place a coil on each 24-gauge wire piece, and bring the coils to the exact center of each wire piece.

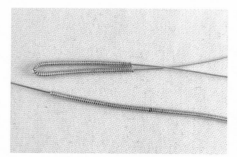

11 Bend the coiled wire precisely in half.

12 Repeat with the second coiled wire piece.

wire art jewelry workshop

13 Flush-cut two pieces of 20-gauge wire, each 5" (12.5 cm) long.

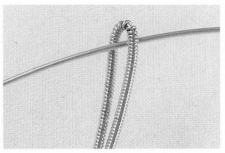

14 Place the coiled wire from Step 11 onto one of the 20-gauge wire pieces.

15 Begin coiling the previously coiled wire onto the 20-gauge wire.

16 Coil the entire length of wire and press down the ends with flat-nose pliers as in Step 4.

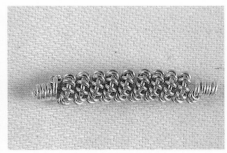

17 Remove the double-coiled wire pieces and set them aside.

18 Place one end of the 20-gauge wire in the middle of the small round-nose pliers.

19 Bend the wire over in a loop as shown, ensuring that the wire touches itself.

20 Use the tips of the round-nose (or chain-nose) pliers to bend the wire back sharply; this is known as "breaking the neck."

21 Reinsert the round-nose pliers into the loop and rock it forward until it resembles a lollipop.

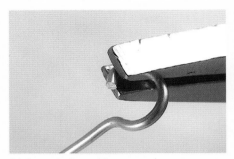

22 Open the loop sideways.

23 Place a bead dangle on the loop.

24 Close the loop sideways.

25 Gather an assortment of small beads, pearls, crystals, found elements, etc., to be used in your earring design. Any size or shape of bead may be used, but all must have holes to accommodate 20-gauge wire.

26 String various beads and a double-coil-wrapped element onto the 20-gauge wire in whatever order you prefer. Your Gypsy Stick earrings can be any length, but I usually keep them about 3" (7.5 cm) long.

27 Grasp the wire in the middle of the round-nose pliers and bend the wire over in a loop.

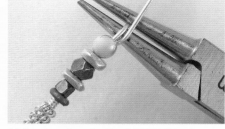

28 Continue bending the wire until you have a closed loop, with the wire flat across the tool.

29 "Break the neck" using round-nose or chain-nose pliers.

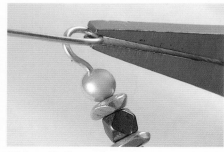

30 Open the loop sideways.

31 Place an ear wire on the loop.

32 Close the loop sideways and place it on round-nose pliers. Place the tool in your left hand, with the wrapping wire to the left and the beaded wire facing directly away from you.

33 Use chain-nose pliers to wrap the wire sharply over to the right.

34 Wrap the wire under and to the left.

wire art jewelry workshop

35 Continue wrapping the wire under and over, wrapping down from the eye-pin loop toward the beaded wire. Stop when you have about ½" (1.3 cm) of straight wire remaining.

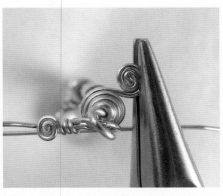

36 Spiral in this wire, starting with round-nose and finishing with chain-nose pliers.

37 Press the spiral firmly against the bead.

Variation:
This is another pair of Gypsy Stick earrings, made with labradorite beads, small silver spacer beads, and coiled wire. The design possibilities are limitless when it comes to these earrings! And you can give them an instantly "aged" look by submerging them in a solution of liver of sulfur. Polish them afterward with superfine steel wool, followed by a jeweler's polishing cloth.

gypsy stick earrings

Angel's EARRINGS

These unusual earrings have several elements that make them stand out: a double-coil-wrapped U-shaped wire piece, handmade French ear wires, bead or pearl dangles, and a double-spiral wire link that holds everything together. Although they are complex and a bit challenging for the beginner to attempt, once they're assembled I think you'll find them well worth the effort.

materials

- 12 small beads
- 2 French ear wires
- 2 bead dangles on head pins
- Round dead-soft wire: 4' (122 cm) 24-gauge, 14" (35.5 cm) 22-gauge, 6" (15 cm) 20-gauge, 10" (25.5 cm) 18-gauge

tools

- Flush cutters
- Ruler, tape measure
- Jewelry pliers: small round-nose, chain-nose, flat-nose, and bail-forming
- 0000 (superfine) steel wool

 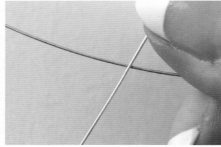 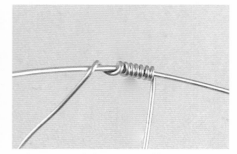

1 Clean all of your wire with 0000 (superfine) steel wool.

2 Prepare to wrap the 24-gauge wire around the 22-gauge wire by crossing the finer gauge on top of the heavier gauge as shown.

3 Bend the 24-gauge wire over the 22-gauge wire and begin wrapping a tight coil. Make every effort to wrap the wire firmly, with each coil lying adjacent to the coil preceding it (no gaps or over-wraps).

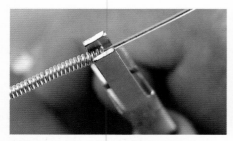  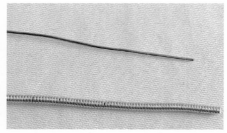

4 When you've wrapped half the wire, press down the wire end firmly using flat-nose pliers. Pull the coil to the opposite end of the 22-gauge wire.

5 Wrap a tight coil as before, and when you come to the end, be sure to press down the wire end very firmly with flat-nose pliers.

6 Remove the coil from the 22-gauge wire.

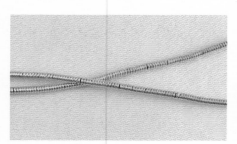 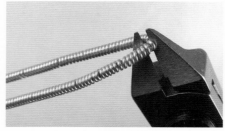 

7 Bend the coil precisely in half.

8 Use flush-cutters to cut the coil precisely in half. Flush-cut the itty-bitty wire end of each coil so they have smooth ends.

9 Flush-cut two 7" (18 cm) pieces of 22-gauge wire. Place a coil onto each 22-gauge wire piece. Use flat-nose pliers to guide the 22-gauge wire into the coil.

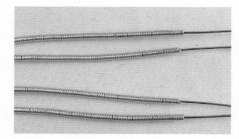  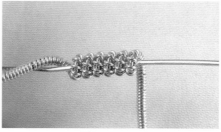

10 Bring the coil to the exact center of each 22-gauge wire piece, with an equal amount of 22-gauge wire protruding from each end of both coils. Bend both coil-wrapped wire pieces precisely in half.

11 Flush-cut two 3" (7.5 cm) pieces of 20-gauge wire and begin wrapping each coil-wrapped wire piece onto a 20-gauge wire piece.

12 You are now forming a double-coiled wire wrap. Be sure to wrap the wire tightly, with no gaps between coils.

wire art jewelry workshop

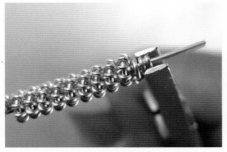

13 When you run out of coiled wire, continue wrapping the bare wire around the 20-gauge wire piece. Press down the wire end with flat-nose pliers.

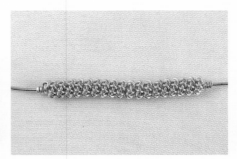

14 Here is the finished double-coil-wrapped wire piece. Bring the coil-wrapped wire to the center of the 20-gauge wire, with an equal amount of 20-gauge wire protruding from each end of the coiled wire.

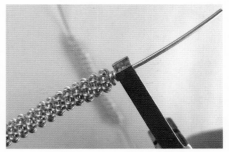

15 You will need two of these for a pair of earrings; again, make sure to press down the wire ends very firmly using flat-nose pliers.

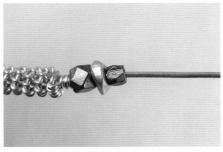

16 Place up to three small beads, pearls, or crystals of your choice on one wire end as shown.

17 Place the wire in the middle (about) of the small round-nose pliers.

18 Bend the wire all the way over until it touches itself.

19 Use the tips of the round-nose (or chain-nose) pliers to bend the wire back sharply. This is known as "breaking the neck."

20 Repeat Steps 16–19 on the opposite end of the 20-gauge wire. Then bend the entire unit in half, forming a U shape. To create a more pleasing U shape, use a tool such as large bail-forming pliers to form it.

21 Lay out your earring elements: two U-shaped coil-wrapped wires, two bead dangles on head pins, and two French ear wires (see the Basic Techniques sections for these two elements).

angel's earrings

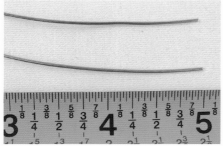

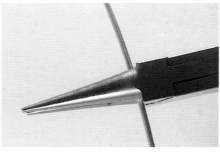

22 The earring elements you've made so far could be joined together with a simple large jump ring. This is an easy solution and it would look great, but if you'd like to add a bit of interest to your design, follow the remaining directions. Start by flush-cutting two 5" (12.5 cm) pieces of 18-gauge wire.

23 Grasp the middle of one 18-gauge wire piece in the back of the small round-nose pliers.

24 Bend both wire ends around the tool, making sure to bend an equal amount of wire on each end so that the round-nose pliers remain in the very center of the wire.

25 Continue bending the wire around the tool until you've created one complete loop.

26 Place a bead dangle on the loop.

27 Open the loop sideways and place a French ear wire on the loop.

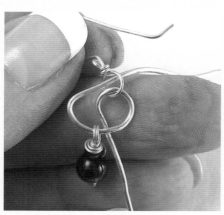

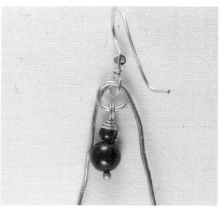

28 Open the loop more so that you can pass the other wire end through the eye-pin loop on the French ear wire. This may distort the loop made in Steps 24–25, but you will be able to reshape the loop.

29 Use the round-nose pliers to reshape the distorted loop.

30 Here is how the unit looks with a French ear wire and bead dangle attached. Again, take special care to keep an equal amount of straight wire coming out on each side of the center loop; this wire will be used to make spirals, and you want each spiral to be identical in size.

wire art jewelry workshop

31 Begin spiraling in one wire end on the tips of the small round-nose pliers. Switch to chain-nose (or flat-nose) pliers and tighten the beginning spiral.

32 Spiral in the wire toward the center loop.

33 Spiral in each wire end until they reach the center loop, making sure that each spiral is identical. Repeat these steps so that you have two earrings ready to be finished with the dangling U-shaped wire pieces made earlier.

34 Open the eye-pin loop on a U-shaped wire piece.

35 Place the eye-pin loop on the center loop on one side of the bead dangle. Close the eye-pin loop securely. Open the second eye-pin loop on the U-shaped wire piece and place it on the other side of the bead dangle. Close it securely.

angel's earrings

A lot of wire is used to make these special earrings, so they tend to be somewhat heavier than usual. For this reason, avoid the temptation to use a lot of beads or heavy, chunky beads in this particular design. Limit yourself to just a few carefully chosen small gemstone beads, crystals, pearls, and/or metal beads. Let the double-coil-wrapped wire remain the star of the show; too many beads will detract from the design.

I recommend using liver of sulfur to darken your earrings as shown in the finished example. This technique really brings out the details of the coil-wrapped wire.

Triangle Drop
EARRINGS

Triangle Drop earrings on handmade French ear hooks can be made in different sizes, with lots of beads or few, in any design that you like. The pattern provided requires making a triangular-shaped frame with 4" (10 cm) of 18-gauge wire, but you can vary this by using more or less wire or wire in lighter gauges. Coil wire in different gauges and metals and use your favorite small beads, spacers, bead caps, crystals, or pearls.

materials

- 4 bead or pearl dangles
- Round dead-soft wire: 12" (30.5 cm) 18-gauge, 12" (30.5 cm) 20-gauge, 18" (45.5 cm) 22-gauge
- Assortment of small beads, spacers, crystals, pearls, etc., of your choice

tools

- Flush cutters
- Ruler, tape measure
- 0000 (superfine) steel wool
- Jewelry pliers: bail-forming, small round-nose, chain-nose, and flat-nose

1 Flush-cut several lengths of wire to coil on the 18-gauge wire. I generally cut 2'–3' (61–91.5 cm) of wire in gauges from 20 to 24 and may or may not use all of the wire that I coil. Clean all of your wire thoroughly with 0000 (superfine) steel wool.

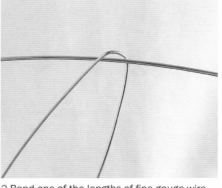

2 Bend one of the lengths of fine-gauge wire over the 18-gauge wire, in preparation for coiling it.

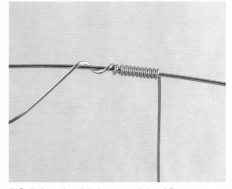

3 Coil the wire tightly around the 18-gauge wire, with no gaps or over-wraps.

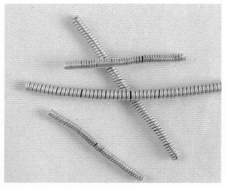

4 When you've coiled several pieces of wire, set them aside. You may or may not use them all in a single pair of earrings; any leftover coils may be used in various other projects.

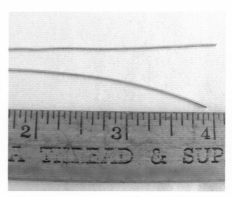

5 Flush-cut two pieces of 18-gauge wire, each 4" (10 cm) long.

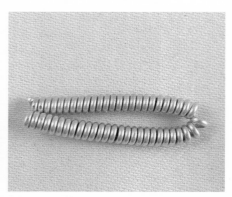

6 Bend the 20-gauge coiled wire in half.

7 Cut the coil at the bend.

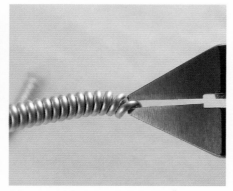

8 Because the coil has been cut on the diagonal, you'll need to flush-cut both coil ends so they have a smooth finish.

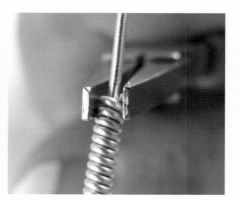

9 Place each coil on a 4" (10 cm) piece of 18-gauge wire and press down the coiled ends if needed.

wire art jewelry workshop

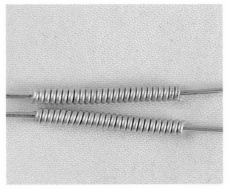

10 Bring each coil to the precise center of each 18-gauge wire piece.

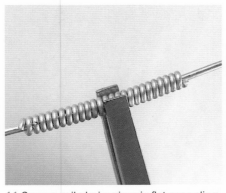

11 Grasp a coiled wire piece in flat-nose pliers, just to the right of center.

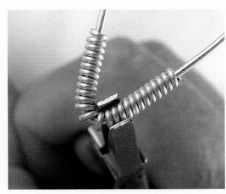

12 Bend the wire at a sharp angle as shown.

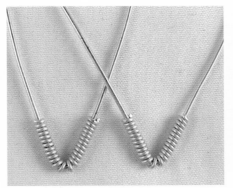

13 Here is how the two coiled wire pieces should look.

14 Place the two largest bead dangles on the coiled wire pieces.

15 Start stringing the wires with beads, small bead caps, spacer beads, crystals, etc., (your choice of small beads).

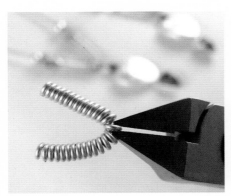

16 Grasp another coiled wire piece, either 22-gauge wire or 24-gauge, and bend it in half. Cut the coil in half and then in half again so that you have four coiled wire pieces of equal length.

17 String the coiled wire pieces onto the 18-gauge wire shape, reserving about ½" (1.3 cm) of bare wire on each end to use in the next steps.

18 Bend small loops with the bare wire ends, in the middle of the small round-nose pliers. Note that each loop is facing the same direction.

triangle drop earrings

19 "Break the neck" using the tips of the chain-nose pliers.

20 Straighten the eye-pin loops if necessary using the round-nose pliers.

21 Use flat-nose pliers to bend a sharp angle in the coiled wire as shown. Bend the eye-pin loops toward each other.

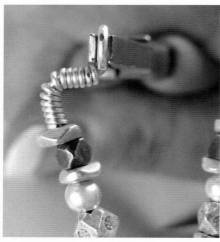

22 Bend the eye-pin loops straight up. Repeat Steps 21–22 with the second eye-pin loop.

23 Place the triangle shape on your work surface with a small bead dangle. This is the earring pattern, which will be connected with a French ear hook.

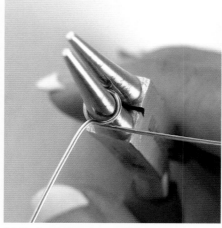

24 Flush-cut two pieces of 22-gauge wire, each 3" (7.5 cm) long. Pick up each piece separately and make eye-pin loops (see the Basic Techniques section). Stop before wrapping the loops.

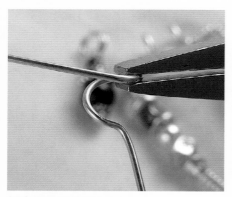

25 Open a loop sideways.

26 Run the wire through one eye-pin loop on the triangle-shaped wire piece, then through the small bead dangle, followed by the second eye-pin loop on the triangle-shaped wire piece.

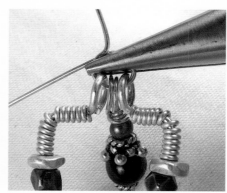

27 Close the loop sideways, pressing firmly.

wire art jewelry workshop

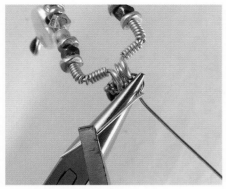

28 Begin wrapping the eye-pin loop.

29 Wrap the wire a second time.

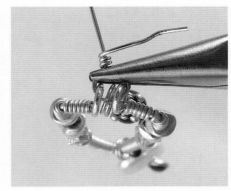

30 When you've wrapped three times, stop.

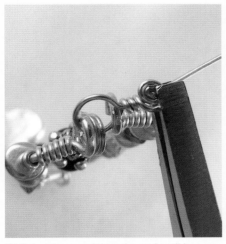

31 Spiral the remaining wire end until it meets the straight wire.

32 Using flat-nose pliers, bend the straight wire over the spiral.

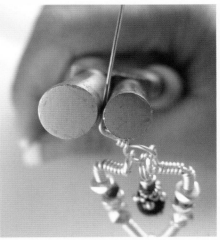

33 Grasp the wire with either large bail-forming pliers (shown) or large round-nose pliers.

34 Bend the wire over the tool to form a shepherd's hook shape.

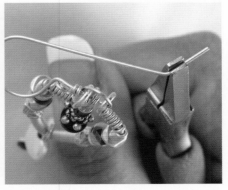

35 To finish, bend back the tail end of the ear hook. As an option, you may want to file the wire end to smooth the end. The ear hook also may be hammered with a plastic mallet to work-harden it.

triangle drop earrings

Squiggle EARRINGS

materials

- 2 bead dangles
- Round dead-soft wire: 14" (35.5 cm) 20-gauge

tools

- Flush cutters
- Ruler, tape measure
- 0000 (superfine) steel wool
- Jewelry pliers: small round-nose, chain-nose, flat-nose, and bail-forming

Wire "squiggles" provide the basic structure for these free-form post earrings. You'll notice that each one is different, but they have two unifying similarities: The same amount of wire was used to form each earring, ensuring a fairly equal size, and an identical bead dangle suspends from each ear wire. This combination of unity and variation creates a harmonious and creative alternative to the usual perfectly matched earring design. Your earrings may be quite different, and it's easy to vary them further by using more wire or by adding more bead dangles in different positions.

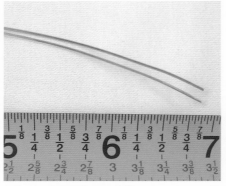

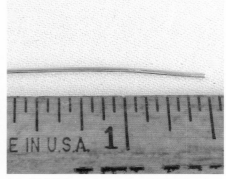

1 Clean your wire thoroughly with 0000 (superfine) steel wool.

2 Flush-cut two pieces of 20-gauge wire, each 7" (18 cm) long.

3 At 1½" (3.8 cm) from one end of each wire piece, bend a sharp, 90-degree angle in the wire.

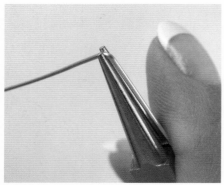

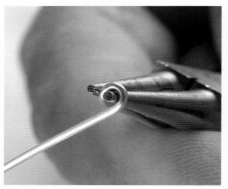

4 Place the bent wire in the tips of the small round-nose pliers as shown, with the shorter wire length running down the tool. Hold this wire end firmly with your index finger.

5 Pressing your left thumb against the outer edge of the wire, turn the round-nose pliers in your hand to form a tiny loop. This loop will be enlarged into a spiral that is at a 90-degree angle to the 1½" (3.8 cm) long wire end from Step 3.

6 Grasp the beginning spiral in the tips of the chain-nose pliers.

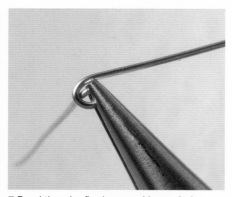

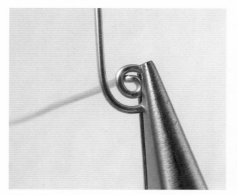

7 Bend the wire firmly around in a spiral.

8 Continue spiraling the wire, always grasping the edge of the spiral in the chain-nose (or flat-nose) pliers. Note that this spiral is rather loose; your spiral can be loose or tight, as this is a personal choice.

9 Once you've spiraled the wire around a couple of times, change the position of the round-nose pliers to start bending the wire in a new direction.

wire art jewelry workshop

10 Holding the pliers still, use your fingers to grasp the wire end and pull it around the tool.

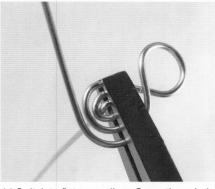

11 Switch to flat-nose pliers. Grasp the spiral and bend the wire around the outer edge of it, or in any direction you choose.

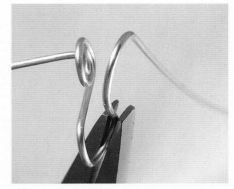

12 Open the loop (created in Step 10) sideways.

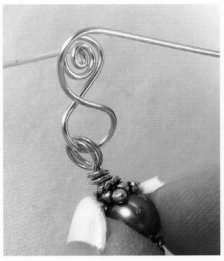

13 Place a bead- or pearl-dangle on the loop and close it sideways.

14 Use the round-nose pliers to continue shaping the wire as desired. Various designs are possible.

15 By changing the position of the pliers, you can shape the wire any way you'd like it to go.

16 Here you can see that the wire is ready to be shaped in another new direction.

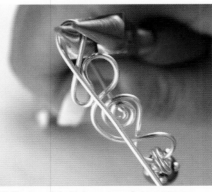

17 Back and forth in series of zigzag loops and back up again.

18 The size and shape of the loops and other wire forms you create with your tools is entirely up to you. This is a free-form design, created as you go.

squiggle earrings

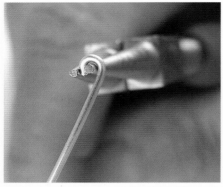

19 When you have about 2"–3" (5–7.5 cm) of straight wire left, it's time to start thinking about spiraling it. Always start your spirals in the tips of the small round-nose pliers.

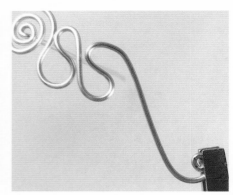

20 Use flat-nose (or chain-nose) pliers to tighten down the beginning spiral.

21 Spiral in the wire.

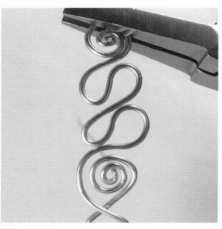

22 Keep spiraling until you reach the shaped wire piece.

23 Here is the finished design. Remember, your design can be completely different. This is your opportunity to express yourself creatively!

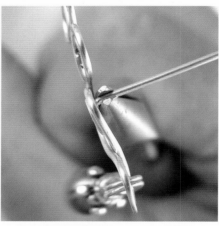

24 To form an ear wire, first grasp the wire protruding at a 90-degree angle from the looped design. Use chain-nose pliers for this, because they have fine tips that won't mar the wire.

25 Bend the wire straight up against the edge of the tool. Note the direction the wire is pointing: away from the bead dangle.

26 Take hold of the wire in the jaws of large bail-forming pliers.

27 Use the smaller (6.8 mm) jaw of the bail-forming pliers to form the ear wire. Press the wire firmly against the tool with your fingertips.

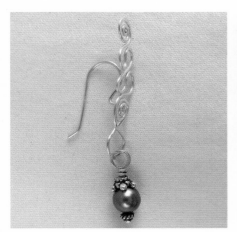

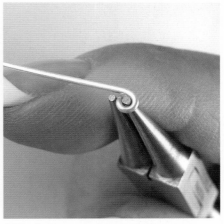

28 Bend the last ⅛" (3 mm) of wire up just a bit to make it easier to insert the earring into your earlobe. Filing the end with a fine jeweler's file is not a bad idea.

29 Here is how the finished earring looks after it has been hammered just a bit with a chasing hammer, an optional step. Note that only the outer edges of the loops and spirals have been hammered.

30 Begin the second earring in the same way as in Steps 4–5.

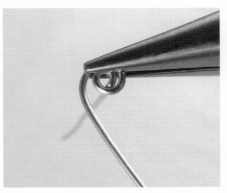

31 Spiral the wire around loosely as shown.

32 Grasp the wire in a new position, in the middle of the round-nose pliers.

33 Bend a loop in the wire by wrapping it tightly around the tool.

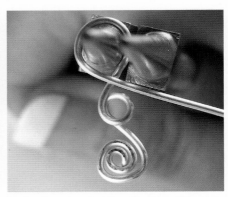

34 Continue bending the wire around to form a tiny decorative loop.

35 Grasp the wire in the back of the round-nose pliers in order to bend the wire in a new direction.

36 Continue bending the wire around the tool.

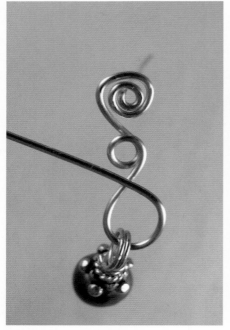

37 Once you've formed a loop, add a bead- or pearl-dangle of your choice.

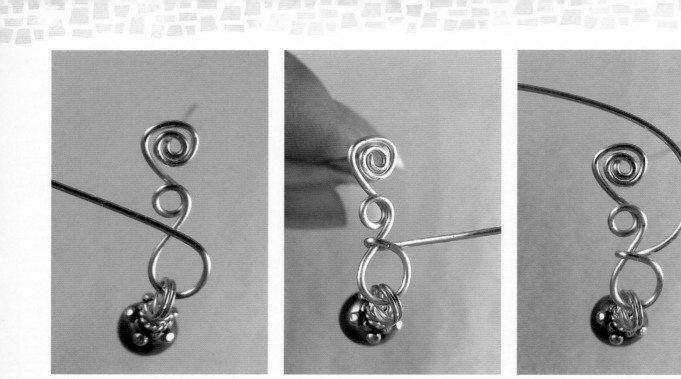

38 Wrap the wire tightly around itself.

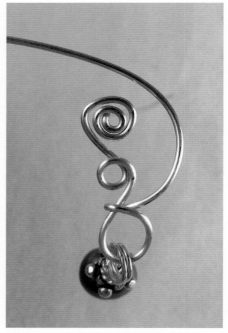

39 Use your fingertips to shape the wire in a wide arc around the top spiral.

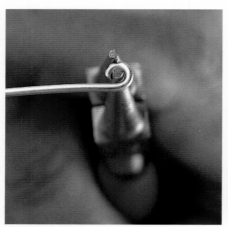

40 Start a small spiral in the end of the wire, using the tips of the small round-nose pliers as before.

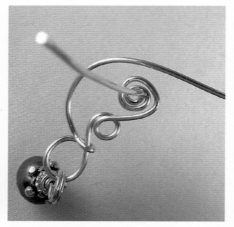

41 Spiral the wire in loosely, using either chain-nose or flat-nose pliers.

42 Shape the wire and place the spiral wherever you want it to end. Hammering the finished earring shape gently with a chasing hammer will add texture; this is an optional step.

wire art jewelry workshop

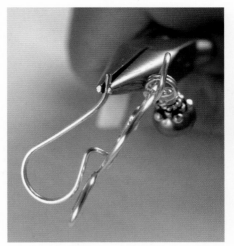

43 Shape the ear wire on the back of the earring as described in Steps 24–28.

squiggle earrings

My "squiggle" wire design for earrings opens up many options for creativity in jewelry making, so please don't feel compelled to follow the instructions provided here in every detail. Where I have "zigged" you might want to "zag," so to speak! Have fun with it, and take the wire where it seems to want to go. When creating free-form organic designs, the wire may "speak" to you and have its own ideas about how it wants to be shaped. If you run out of ideas, try my "blind-design" technique:

Pick up a scrap piece of 20-gauge wire about 8" (20 cm) to 10" (25 cm) long. Close your eyes and start shaping the wire with your fingers. Let the wire dictate its direction. Keep your eyes closed as you pick up round-nose or chain-nose pliers and use them to shape the wire. Wrap, spiral, coil, bend, and twist the wire piece, all the while keeping your eyes firmly

shut. When you've run out of straight wire to play with, open your eyes. Wow, you just made something new and original!

Note that the earring pair I made for the sample provided is not perfectly symmetrical. In fact, each earring is quite different from its mate, but they seem to go together rather well, don't they? The secret to balancing this asymmetrical design is to use the same amount of wire for each earring, even though they are shaped differently. Also use identical bead or pearl dangles as shown in the sample pair. The eye craves unity in design, but it also delights in variety, so by providing both concepts in one pair of earrings you are sure to end up with a pleasing design.

You might also want to try my blind-design technique to make shaped wire links instead of earrings.

Snake Vertebrae
EARRINGS

This pair of earrings has the look of a jointed spine with a bead or pearl dangle suspended from the "tail" end. These earrings may look complex, but they're not very difficult or time-consuming to make. And they're certainly unusual! Because only a small amount of wire was used to make them, they're lightweight and very comfortable to wear.

materials

- 2 French ear wires
- 4 small jump rings
- 2 bead or pearl dangles
- Round dead-soft wire: 2' (61 cm) 18-gauge

tools

- Ruler
- Flush cutters
- 0000 (superfine) steel wool
- Jewelry pliers: small round-nose, chain-nose, flat-nose, and bail-forming

1 Clean all of your wire with 0000 (superfine) steel wool. Gather your materials: For two earrings, you will need two French ear wires (see the Basic Techniques section) or the commercial ear wires of your choice; four small (6mm outer diameter) jump rings made with 18-gauge wire; and two bead or pearl dangles on commercial or handmade head pins. You will also need flush-cut 18-gauge wire in the following lengths: two pieces 5" (12.5 cm) long, two pieces 4" (10 cm) long, and two pieces 3" (7.5 cm) long.

2 Pick up a 5" (12.5 cm) wire piece, grasping the middle of the wire in the middle of the small round-nose pliers. Note: It's critically important to grasp the wire precisely in the middle.

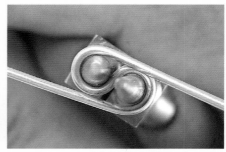

3 Holding the pliers still, bend the wire around both jaws of the tool, bending in the same direction to form a "yin-yang" shape.

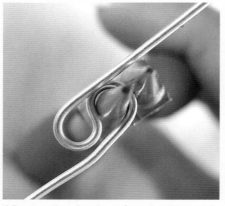

4 Remove the wire shape from the pliers, and replace the tool with the bottom jaw in the top loop.

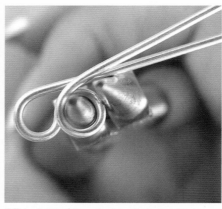

5 Take hold of the wire hanging straight down, and bend it up firmly against the tool.

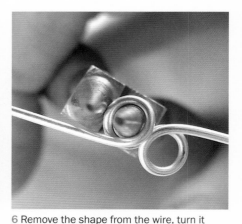

6 Remove the shape from the wire, turn it over, and replace the tool with the bottom jaw in the top loop.

Take hold of the wire hanging straight down, and bend it up firmly against the tool.

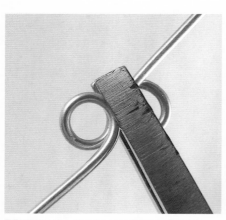

7 Remove the round-nose pliers and gently press the center of the shaped wire with either flat-nose or chain-nose pliers.

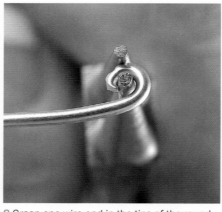

8 Grasp one wire end in the tips of the round-nose pliers and bend a tiny loop.

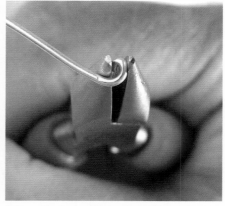

9 Close the loop with the tips of the chain-nose pliers.

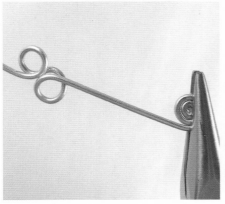

10 Use chain-nose or flat-nose pliers to spiral in the wire toward the two loops.

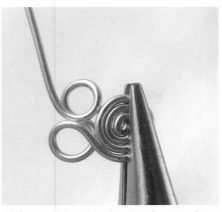

11 Stop spiraling the wire when it meets the two loops right in the center.

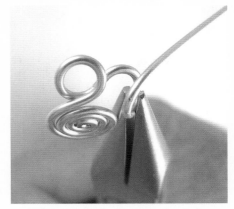

12 Before spiraling in the other wire end, open up its loop sideways using either chain-nose or flat-nose pliers.

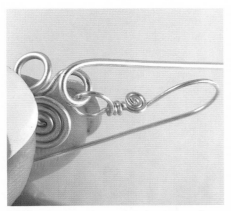

13 Place an ear wire on the wire and run it down until it hangs on the loop.

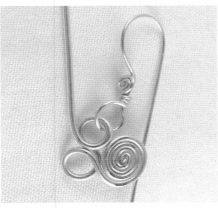

14 Close the loop sideways. Note the correct orientation of the ear wire to the shaped wire link.

15 Follow Steps 9–12 to spiral in the remaining straight wire on the shaped link.

16 Here is the finished link suspended from the ear wire.

17 Follow the same steps outlined above with the 4" (10 cm) wire piece to make an identical (but smaller) shaped wire link. This link does not have anything attached to it.

18 Pick up the 3" (7.5 cm) wire piece and shape it following Steps 2–12.

snake vertebrae earrings

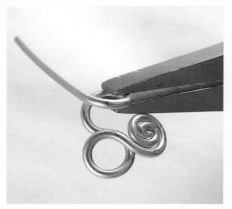

19 Before spiraling in the other wire end, open up its loop sideways using either chain-nose or flat-nose pliers.

20 Place a bead or pearl dangle on the wire, and run it down the wire until it hangs on the loop.

21 Close the loop sideways.

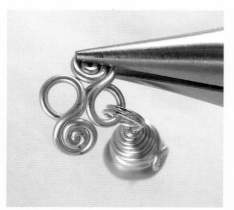

22 Follow Steps 9–12 to spiral in the remaining straight wire on the shaped link.

23 Lay out your materials on your work surface in the pattern shown. Condition two 6mm jump rings and open them in preparation for using them to connect all the elements together.

24 Open a jump ring sideways and run it through the top loop on the smallest shaped wire link, with the bead or pearl dangle suspended below.

wire art jewelry workshop

25 Pick up the middle shaped wire link and run the open jump ring through both loops as shown.

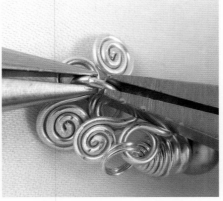

26 Use flat-nose and chain-nose pliers to close the jump ring securely.

27 This is how it should look so far.

28 Open the second jump ring sideways and run it through the top loop on the middle shaped wire link.

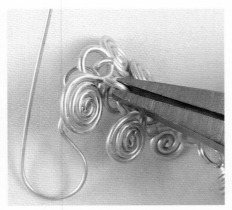

29 Pick up the largest shaped wire link and run the open jump ring through both loops as shown.

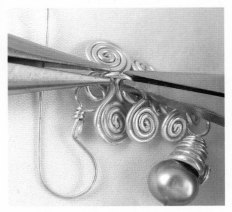

30 Use flat-nose and chain-nose pliers to close the jump ring securely.

snake vertebrae earrings

I've enjoyed making these earrings in both sterling silver and copper wire. Many variations on this design are possible. Why not try making your earrings in mixed metals? For example, the largest link could be made using sterling silver wire, the middle link made from copper wire, and the smallest link made from yellow brass or gold-filled wire. Or you could make your links much bigger than the ones I made for the sample earrings. You might also try using just one of the links to dangle from an ear wire and dangle something different beneath that. For example, a big wire spiral that's been flattened and textured—or any other shaped wire piece—or a cluster of tiny beads or pearls, or a found object, or some other little trinket. The possibilities!

Bird's Nest
BANGLE

This complex-looking bracelet design begins with a simple overhand knot. From there, it's crafted by tying a string of knots onto the preceding ones. Because making the bangle requires a fair amount of hand manipulation, it's important to use dead-soft round wire. Try making your bracelet with a variety of different gauges—14-gauge, 16-gauge, and/or 18-gauge—in silver or copper wire. Soon you'll have a tangled "bird's nest" of wire to wear on your wrist.

materials

- Round dead-soft wire: 4' (122 cm) 14-gauge, 4' (122 cm) 16-gauge, optional 4' (122 cm) 18-gauge

tools

- Flush cutters
- Tape measure
- Bracelet mandrel
- Hard-plastic mallet
- Small steel bench block
- 0000 (superfine) steel wool
- Chasing hammer with a convex face
- Jewelry pliers: round-nose, chain-nose, and flat-nose

1 Clean your wire thoroughly with 0000 (superfine) steel wool.

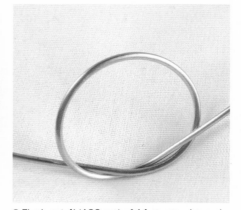

2 Flush-cut 4' (122 cm) of 14-gauge wire and tie a loose overhand knot in the center.

3 Manipulate the knot in your fingers and bring the wire on the right up and through any one of the loops created in the original knot. Pull it firmly. For the time being, leave the wire on the left hanging loose (until you get to Step 13).

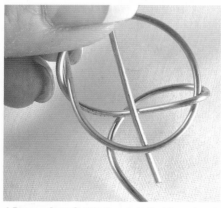

4 Repeat Step 3, this time bringing the wire end up and through another loop in the developing design. Notice that the wire is coming down, and, as it passes through a loop, it first goes over one wire and then under the next one.

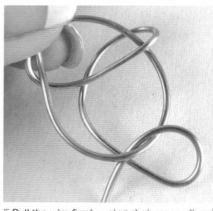

5 Pull the wire firmly, using chain-nose pliers if necessary.

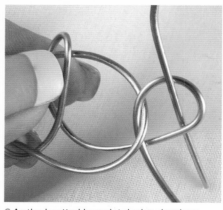

6 As the knotted bracelet design develops, continue tying loose knots of wire by running the wire down through previous loops. As you design the bracelet, consider how you want it to appear—a wide band with large loops, or a narrow band with tighter loops.

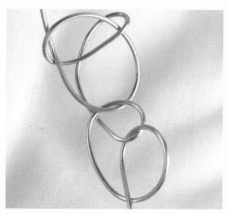

7 Here you can see how the design is coming along, with a series of loosely tied overhand knots all moving in one direction to form a fairly wide band.

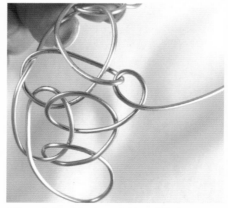

8 To make a wider bracelet band, tie large knots of wire along both sides of the original design.

9 Once the knotted band is about 5" (12.5 cm) long, place it on the bracelet mandrel to shape it. Use a hard-plastic mallet to gently hammer the wire, but take care not to hammer very much or the crossed wires could break.

wire art jewelry workshop

10 When you have about 5" (12.5 cm) of straight wire left on one end of the bracelet, forge the very end with a chasing hammer on a bench block.

11 Use round-nose pliers to start a tiny loop at the end of the wire.

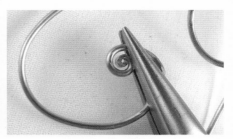

12 Switch to chain-nose (or flat-nose) pliers and spiral in the wire, very loosely. This big spiral will become the hook portion of the clasp on this bracelet.

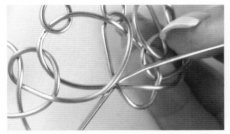

13 Pick up the other wire end that was left at Step 3. You should have about 2' (61 cm) of 14-gauge wire to work with; simply tie loose overhand knots as before to continue fashioning the knotted bangle.

14 Finish this end of the bracelet with one very large loop and wrap the last 2" (5 cm) of wire around itself using pliers as needed. This end forms the "eye" portion of the clasp on the bracelet.

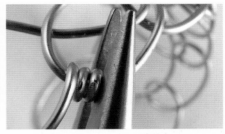

15 Use chain-nose pliers to press down the wire end.

16 Place the bracelet back on the mandrel and hammer it into shape with a hard-plastic mallet. Take care not to overdo this, especially where any wires cross.

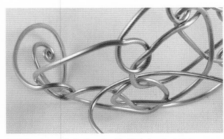

17 The bangle is basically finished at this point, but as an option, you may add more wire to it in a finer gauge. Bend a 4' (122 cm) piece of 16-gauge wire in half and run the wire through any part of the bangle until you reach the halfway point.

18 If you look at the very center of the picture, you'll see where the new wires have been crossed and are now permanently attached to the developing bangle.

19 Tie knots of 16-gauge wire onto the bangle as before, this time pulling the knots tighter with the aid of the chain-nose pliers.

20 See how tightly you can pull the knots by using pliers instead of your bare fingers. Keep in mind that the 16-gauge wire is being used as embellishment on the finished bangle. Tie on as much or as little as you like and finish each end by spiraling in the wire. Try on the bangle to see if it fits. If it needs to be lengthened, this is easy to do by adding more wire loops to either end and making alterations to the loop-end of the clasp.

bird's nest bangle

Cage Bead
BRACELET

In the Basic Techniques section, I showed how to make cage beads with 16-gauge round wire. Once you've made several cage beads, they can be used with other beads and wire links in various jewelry pieces. Or you can try making a handful of cage beads in different sizes and creating a bracelet based on them.

materials

- 16–20 large jump rings
- Cage beads in various sizes with eye-pin links inserted

tools

- Jewelry pliers: bail-forming, bent chain-nose, and flat-nose
- 0000 (superfine) steel

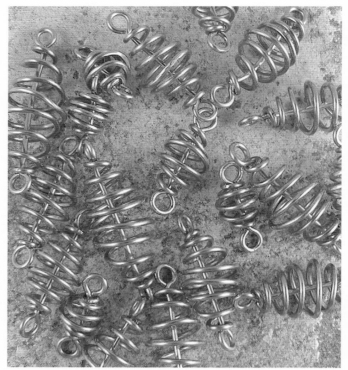

2 Create large jump rings using the smaller (6.8 mm) jaw on bail-forming pliers. Close all jump rings.

1 Assemble an assortment of cage beads with eye-pin link connectors as demonstrated in the Basic Techniques section (p. 28). To make cage beads in different sizes, simply use more or less wire to create each cage. The beads in the bracelet were made with 16-gauge round dead-soft copper wire in the following lengths: 4" (10 cm), 5" (12.5 cm), 6" (15 cm), 7" (18 cm), 8" (20.5 cm), and 9" (23 cm).

3 Open and insert a jump ring through a closed one. Close it securely.

4 Make several (eight to ten or so) doubled jump ring sets and set them aside.

5 Open the eye-pin loop on a cage bead sideways.

6 Insert the opened eye-pin loop through a doubled jump ring set.

wire art jewelry workshop

7 Close the eye-pin loop sideways and press it firmly.

8 Continue linking cage beads with doubled jump rings in a pleasing pattern, varying the sizes of the cage beads.

9 Finish by connecting the two bracelet ends with doubled jump rings. As an option, you may add a commercial clasp.

10 The finished bracelet as shown is worn by rolling it over your hand and onto your wrist. It's very comfortable to wear and has a simple, understated elegance. As an attractive option, you can try artificially aging the bracelet in a hot solution of liver of sulfur. Clean and polish the metal with 0000 (superfine) steel wool and throw the bracelet in a jewelry tumbler for half an hour to bring up the shine.

cage bead bracelet

Snake Vertebrae
BRACELET

This slinky bracelet resembles the spine of a snake, the way it drapes nicely on the wrist and curves in a sinuous design. Light and comfortable to wear, it looks great in sterling silver, copper, or brass wire. A handmade hook clasp provides the finishing touch.

materials

- Round dead-soft 16-gauge wire (copper, silver or brass), about 9' (2.74 m)

tools

- Flush cutters
- Small jeweler's file
- Ruler, tape measure
- Small steel bench block
- 0000 (superfine) steel wool
- Chasing hammer with a convex face
- Jewelry pliers: large round-nose, small round-nose, chain-nose, bent chain-nose, flat-nose

1 Clean your wire thoroughly with 0000 (superfine) steel wool or use jewelry polishing pads or cloths.

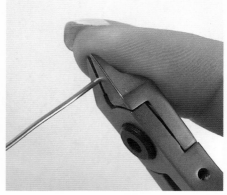

2 Flush-cut the end of 16-gauge wire.

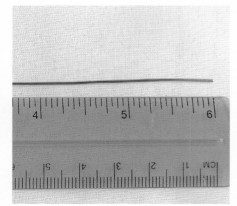

3 Flush-cut at least fourteen 6" (15 cm) pieces (for an 8" (20.5) long bracelet).

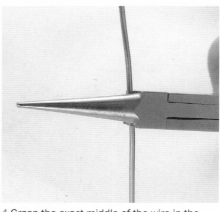

4 Grasp the exact middle of the wire in the back of the small round-nose pliers right next to (but not inside) the box-joint.

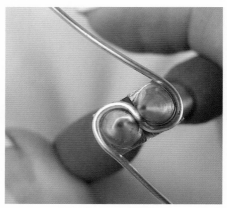

5 Bend the wire in the same direction around the jaws of the pliers.

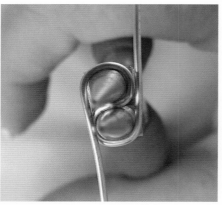

6 Continue bending the wire in the same direction until you have created a yin-yang shape.

7 Remove the wire from the tool and insert the bottom jaw into the top loop. Bring the wire all the way to the back of the tool, right next to the box-joint.

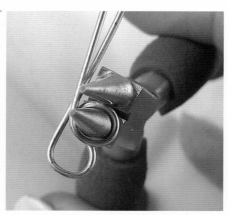

8 Use your fingers to wrap the wire firmly around the tool until both wires are standing straight up.

9 Remove the wire shape from the tool, turn it upside down, and insert the bottom jaw of the tool into the top loop.

wire art jewelry workshop

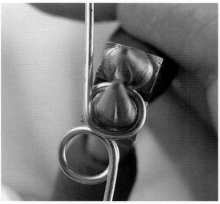

10 Use your fingers to bend the longest wire around the tool so that it points in the opposite direction to the slightly shorter wire.

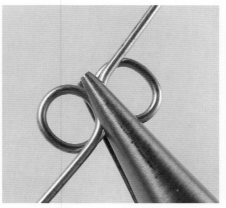

11 Remove the wire from the tool and gently squeeze the center of the wire shape in the tips of the chain-nose pliers.

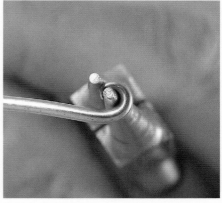

12 Take hold of one wire end in the tips of the small round-nose pliers and bend a tiny loop in the wire.

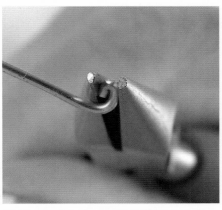

13 Use the tips of chain-nose pliers to gently press the loop tightly closed.

Begin spiraling in the wire.

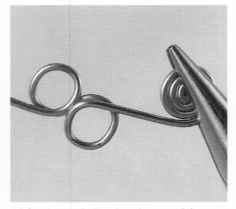

14 Continue spiraling the wire toward the two loops.

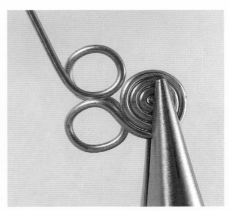

15 Stop spiraling the wire when it meets the spot between the two loops.

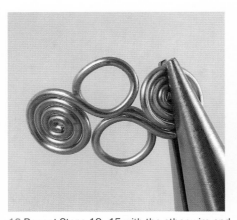

16 Repeat Steps 12–15 with the other wire end.

17 Make several of these double-spiral links and place two together, the one on the left overlapping the one on the right.

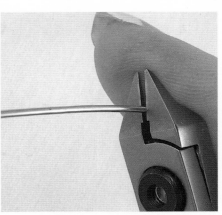

18 Flush-cut some additional 16-gauge wire in preparation for making small jump rings to connect the links into a bracelet.

snake vertebrae bracelet

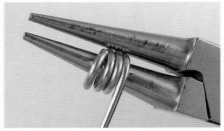

19 Create a coil for at least twenty-six small jump rings in the middle of the small round-nose pliers; finished jump rings should have an outer diameter of 5 mm.

20 Flush-cut and condition your jump rings as described in the Basic Techniques section (p. 50). Open one jump ring sideways and insert it into two double-spiral links as shown.

21 Close the jump ring securely with flat-nose and bent chain-nose pliers.

22 Lay the two links together to see how the pattern will look.

23 Use a second jump ring to connect the double-spiral links.

24 Close this jump ring securely.

25 You can see how the two jump rings hold the two links together securely in a bracelet pattern.

26 Continue linking all of the double-spiral links until you have a bracelet long enough to fit your wrist.

27 Flush-cut a 2" (5 cm) piece of 16-gauge wire.

28 Hammer the wire end with a chasing hammer to thin it down just a bit.

29 Begin bending the wire end in the tips of the small round-nose pliers.

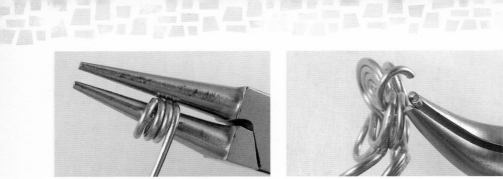

30 Use flat-nose pliers to gently tighten the loop.

31 Spiral in the wire just a tiny bit.

32 Turn the spiral up, facing yourself, and place it in the very back of the larger round-nose pliers, right up against (but not inside) the box-joint.

33 Bend the tool up and over to create a hook shape.

34 Use small round-nose pliers to bend another loop in the straight end of the wire.

35 Lightly hammer the back of the hook shape with a chasing hammer.

36 Open the hook's bottom loop sideways.

37 Place the hook on one end of the bracelet.

38 Close the loop. To finish the bracelet, dip it in a hot solution of liver of sulfur, rinse in plain water, dry it with a paper towel, and polish with 0000 (superfine) steel wool and jewelry polishing cloths.

snake vertebrae bracelet

Faux 4-in-1
BRACELET

This bracelet closely resembles a chain-mail pattern called European 4-in-1, but it's actually quite different. Made of heavy (12-gauge) wire, each link is a figure-eight that's been forged and textured and then assembled with jump rings and a unique double-hook clasp. The clasp "disappears" in the jewelry design as you wear it, which is a nice feature. The advantage to making a chain-mail–like bracelet with figure-eight links instead of jump rings is that this type of link is easy to hammer flat and texture with ball-peen or embossing hammers. Try doing that with jump rings, as in a typical European 4-in-1 design! Not so easy.

materials

- Round dead-soft wire (copper or silver): 6' (183 cm) 12-gauge, 3' (91.5 cm) 14-gauge, 1' (30.5 cm) 16-gauge

tools

- Flush cutters
- Hard-plastic mallet
- Ruler, tape measure
- Small steel bench block
- Small embossing hammer
- 0000 (superfine) steel wool
- Chasing hammer with a convex face
- Jewelry pliers: small round-nose, bail-forming, bent chain-nose, and flat-nose

1 Clean the wire thoroughly with 0000 (superfine) steel wool.

2 Flush-cut the wire, holding your finger over the protruding wire end to keep the little bit from flying away and hitting someone.

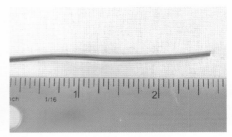

3 Measure and flush-cut 2¾" (7 cm) of 12-gauge wire.

4 Place the wire in the large bail-forming pliers with the largest (8.8 mm) jaw facing away from you. Feel the wire end to make sure it's not protruding above the jaws of the pliers.

5 Roll the tool over in your hand until the wire is wrapped tightly all the way around the largest jaw on the pliers, touching itself.
Repeat to form a perfect figure-eight with the wire.

6 Hammer the figure-eight link with a hard-plastic or rawhide mallet.

7 Forge the outer edge of the figure-eight with a chasing hammer, avoiding other areas of the link.

8 Close up the circle if it opens up during the forging process. Repeat Step 7 on the opposite end of the figure-eight.

9 Use either the ball-peen end of the chasing hammer or a small embossing hammer to add dimpled texture to the flattened areas of the wire. Avoid striking any other part of the link. Repeat Steps 3–8 to make twenty-five or more figure-eight links for an 8" (20.5 cm) long bracelet. Set the links aside.

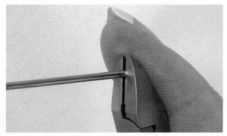

10 Clean and flush-cut the end of some 14-gauge wire; you'll need about 3' (91.5 cm) to make enough jump rings for this bracelet.

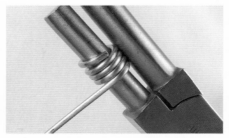

11 Form jump rings on the smaller (6.8 mm) jaw of the large bail-forming pliers. If you need additional help making jump rings, the technique is stepped out in the Basic Techniques section.

12 Flush-cut and condition your jump rings. Place two figure-eight links on your work surface, the one on the right overlapping the one on the left. Open one jump ring sideways.

wire art jewelry workshop

13 Run the jump ring through the midsection of both figure-eight links as shown.

14 Close the jump ring securely using chain-nose or bent chain-nose and flat-nose pliers.

15 Slide the top figure-eight link over to the right to see the pattern.

16 Connect a third figure-eight link to the second figure-eight link as shown.

17 Slide the top figure-eight links to the right to see the pattern.

18 Continue connecting figure-eight links to one another in the same pattern. Close all jump rings very securely.

19 You can see how the bracelet is going to look once it's finished.

20 As you proceed, try the bracelet on for size to determine how many more links must be attached. Reserve one figure-eight link to make into a clasp before attaching it to the bracelet.

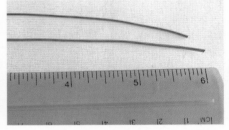

21 Clean and flush-cut two 6" (15 cm) pieces of 16-gauge wire.

22 Bend the wire in half using flat-nose pliers.

23 Use flat-nose pliers to press the wires closely together.

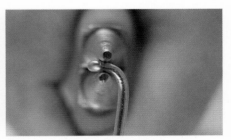

24 Bend the bent end of each wire piece forward using the tips of the round-nose pliers.

faux 4-in-1 bracelet

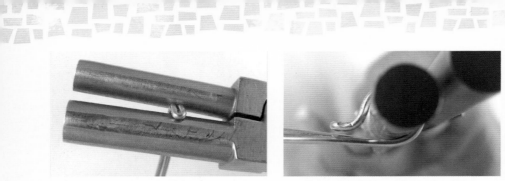

25 Turn the bent wire end toward yourself and place the wire in the large bail-forming pliers with the smallest (6.8 mm) jaw facing away from you.

26 Turn the tool around, carrying the wires with it to form a hook shape. Repeat Steps 23–27 with the second 6" (15 cm) wire piece.

27 Pick up one reserved figure-eight link and place the hook on it as shown. This will help you to visualize the orientation of the hooks on the link.

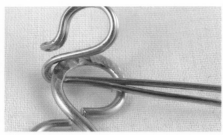

28 Remove the figure-eight link and bend the wire just beneath the hook straight back as shown.

29 Replace the hook back on the figure-eight link.

30 Begin wrapping the wires around the figure-eight link quite firmly.

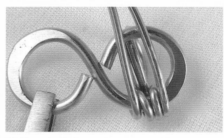

31 In this photo, you see both wires wrapped one complete time around the figure-eight link.

32 Turn the link over to the backside.

33 Use small round-nose pliers to begin a tiny spiral in one wire end.

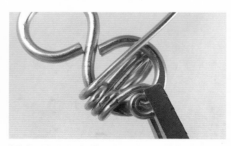

34 Tighten the beginning spiral with flat-nose pliers.

35 Continue spiraling the wire until it meets the figure-eight link.

36 Repeat these steps with the second wrapped wire.

37 Turn the figure-eight link over to expose the front side.

38 Repeat Steps 28–37 with the second 6" (15 cm) wire piece to create a double-hook clasp for the bracelet.

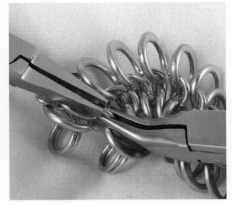

39 Connect the figure-eight link with clasp to the bracelet using a jump ring.

faux 4-in-1 bracelet

When made well, this bracelet drapes beautifully on the wrist. It's a real showpiece, and the simplicity of its design lends itself to many wardrobe choices, from simple tops and jeans to elegant dresses.

To dress it up more, make it using sterling silver, fine silver, or gold-filled wire instead of copper. Hammer out the links as demonstrated, but don't texture the flattened surfaces. This will result in a much more polished, elegant look.

While the finished bracelet looks great when made with heavy-gauge wire as shown in the sample piece, it's quite heavy to wear. Some people prefer not to wear heavy jewelry. So consider making your bracelet using 16-gauge or even 18-gauge instead of 12-gauge wire.

The double clasp on this bracelet is rather unusual, and it's somewhat challenging to make. I designed it so that the bracelet will lie flat on your wrist and drape nicely without calling too much attention to the clasp. But if you don't care for it, substitute a simple hook clasp instead, or attach a commercial clasp.

You may need to make more (or fewer) figure-eight links to fashion a Faux 4-in-1 bracelet that fits your wrist. Try it on several times as you are linking it together to determine its correct measurement.

Double-Spiral
BANGLE

Using heavy-gauge wire to form a stiff bangle is not difficult if you use a bracelet mandrel and a hard-plastic mallet to work-harden the metal. Your bangle can be made with either copper or sterling silver wire. I used 12-gauge copper wire as the base and wrapped it with 16-gauge sterling silver wire in the sample shown. Adding a heavy bead dangle to the bottom of the bangle will keep the double-spiral design riding on the top of your wrist, where it shows to greatest advantage.

materials

- 1 large bead
- Round dead-soft wire: 3' (91.5 cm) 12-gauge and 6' (183 cm) 16-gauge

tools

- Flush cutters
- Chasing hammer
- Bracelet mandrel
- Hard-plastic mallet
- Ruler, tape measure
- Small steel bench block
- 0000 (superfine) steel wool
- Jewelry pliers: large round-nose, small round-nose, large bail-forming, chain-nose, and flat-nose

1 Clean all of your wire thoroughly with 0000 (superfine) steel wool.

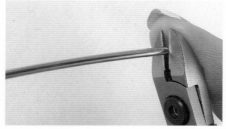

2 Flush-cut 3' (91.5 cm) of 12-gauge round dead-soft wire (copper or silver).

3 Bring the two wire ends together.

4 Fold the wire in half.

5 Place the loop on the largest jaw (8.8 mm) of the large bail-forming pliers. If the wire does not conform well to the tool, as you see in the photo, pull the wire more tightly.

6 Use flat-nose pliers to bend the wire straight up out of the loop.

7 Bend the opposite wire and align the two.

8 Use flat-nose pliers to press the two wires firmly together.

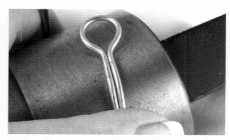

9 Wrap the wire around a bracelet mandrel at your desired placement. *Tip:* Initially it's best to make the bangle one size too large to fit over your hand because in the next several steps you'll be wrapping the two base wires with 16-gauge wire.

10 Hammer the wire on the bracelet mandrel to force it to conform to the round shape. This also work-hardens the wire.

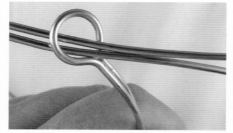

11 Remove the wire from the bracelet mandrel and run the two wire ends through the loop on the opposite end of the wire.

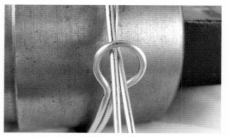

12 Pull the wires through and place the bangle back on the bracelet mandrel.

13 Use flat-nose pliers to pull first one, then the other wire tightly through the loop and around the bracelet mandrel.

14 Hammer the wires gently with a hard-plastic mallet.

15 Hammer each wire end separately on a small steel bench block.

16 Use round-nose pliers to start a small spiral loop on each wire end.

17 Use chain-nose (or flat-nose) pliers to tighten the beginning spiral.

18 Spiral in the wire end using either chain-nose or flat-nose pliers.

19 Repeat Steps 16–18 on the other wire end. Stop both spirals where the bangle begins, as shown.

20 Place the bangle back on the bracelet mandrel.

21 Hammer the bangle gently with a hard-plastic mallet.

22 Use a chasing hammer to flatten the outer edges of both spirals on the bracelet mandrel. Then remove the bangle from the mandrel.

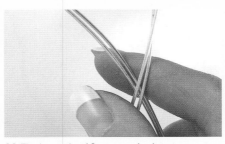

23 Flush cut the 16-gauge wire into two pieces, each 3' (91.5 cm) long.

24 Set one of the wires aside and begin wrapping the other wire around the bangle.

double-spiral bangle

25 As you wrap, periodically stop to press the wrapped wire with flat-nose pliers. This helps to keep the wraps tight and prevent the two bangle wires from twisting as you wrap them.

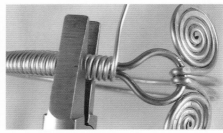

26 Continue wrapping up toward the top of the bangle.

27 When you reach the top of the bangle, trim the wire end a bit if necessary. I trimmed mine to ¾" (2 cm) beyond the outer edge of the bangle, but you could use slightly longer wire for the next steps.

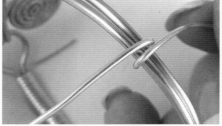

28 Wrap the second 16-gauge wire piece around the bangle, again wrapping toward the top.

29 Once all the wire is wrapped, you should have four short "tails" of wire measuring about ¾"–1" (2–2.5 cm) long each. These will be spiraled in toward the bangle, starting with the tips of the round-nose pliers.

30 Press the beginning spiral firmly to tighten the loop.

31 Continue spiraling in the wire until you reach the top of the bangle.

32 Tuck the spiral firmly against the top of the bangle.

33 Repeat Steps 29–32 with the second wrapped wire. Then spiral in the opposite wire end and press the spirals against the surface of the bangle.

34 Place the bangle back on the mandrel and hammer the outer edges of both spirals with a small embossing hammer.

35 The heaviest item on the bangle is now the spiraled top, and, due to gravity, this is likely to cause the bangle to turn on your wrist until the spirals are beneath your wrist. To prevent this, create a counterweight bead dangle to suspend from the bottom of the bangle. Choose a medium-size but heavy bead and about 8" (20.5 cm) of wire in a gauge that will fit through the bead. Create a spiraled head pin (see the Basic Techniques section for details) and place the bead on it.

36 Wrap a loop on the back of the small round-nose pliers.

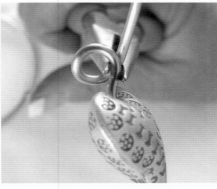

37 "Break the neck" using chain-nose pliers.

38 Open the loop sideways and place the loop on the bangle.

39 Close the loop sideways and begin wrapping the "neck" area between the loop and the bead. In the sample, I used a scrap piece of 12-gauge wire, which was difficult to bend. I suggest using 14-gauge or 16-gauge for your head pin wire, which will be easier to bend. Once you've wrapped the neck, spiral in the end to finish.

40 Here's the finished bangle. To bring out its best features, consider artificially aging it in a hot solution of liver of sulfur.

41 Dip the bracelet in the solution and remove it with a plastic fork. Rinse it in clean water.

42 Dry the bangle thoroughly with a paper towel and polish it with 0000 (superfine) steel wool. Finish with jewelry polishing cloths.

43 The finished antiqued bangle has a completely different look (compare this photo to photo in Step 40).

double-spiral bangle

Celtic Knot
BRACELET

This complex-looking bracelet is a bit unusual because it has no clasp. The obvious advantage to this design is that you'll never have to worry about the clasp coming undone while you wear the bracelet. The disadvantage is that you'll have to work a little harder to make a bracelet that fits properly. Once finished with the design as outlined below, try the bracelet on by rolling it over your wrist. You may need to add or subtract elements to the bracelet until it fits just right.

materials

• 3 Celtic knot links
• 6 rosette jump-ring clusters
• 3 coil-wrapped bead connectors

tools

• Jewelry pliers: bent chain-nose and flat-nose
• 0000 (superfine) steel wool

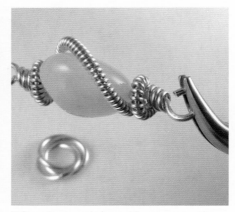

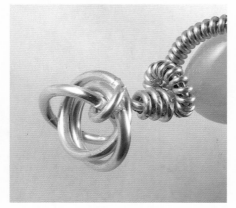

1 Gather your elements for the bracelet as shown. To make coil-wrapped bead connectors, Celtic knot links, and rosette jump-ring clusters, see the Basic Techniques section.

2 Open the eye-pin loop sideways on a coil-wrapped bead connector.

3 Place a rosette jump-ring cluster on the opened eye-pin loop and close the loop sideways.

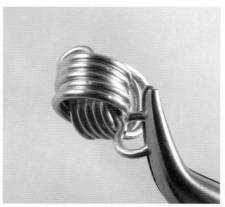

4 Open the eye-pin loop sideways on a Celtic knot link.

5 Attach the rosette jump-ring cluster from Step 3 to the opened eye-pin loop and close the loop sideways.

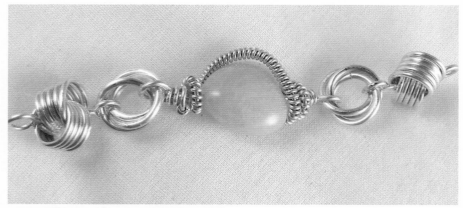

6 Continue connecting coil-wrapped bead connectors with Celtic knot links in this pattern until you have used up all the elements from the materials list. Connect the first and last elements to form a bracelet.

wire art jewelry workshop

7 To finish the bracelet, use a hot solution of liver of sulfur to darken the metal. Polish the jewelry thoroughly with 0000 (superfine) steel wool and use polishing cloths or a jewelry tumbler to bring it to a high shine.

celtic knot bracelet

I purposely designed this bracelet without a clasp. The trouble with bracelet clasps is that they very often ride up on top of your wrist, unless you attach a heavy bead dangle or charm near the clasp to keep this from happening.

I have long wanted to create a bracelet that could roll on and off my wrist without the use of a clasp, but the trouble with this idea is that very often a bracelet that fits over your hand is then too large for your wrist. Or a clasp-less bracelet that fits your wrist is too tight to fit over your hand. The key to success is, as always, experimentation!

Start by making a bracelet with inexpensive copper wire and beads. Try rolling on the finished bracelet. If it goes over your hand and onto your wrist, great.

Now take a look at it. Is it too big? When you dangle your wrist, does the bracelet drape too far down your hand and seem about to slip off? If so, you will need to make adjustments such as using smaller beads to shorten the bracelet, or using fewer Celtic knot links, or connecting the links with smaller jump rings.

If you can't even get the finished bracelet over your wrist, obviously it must be lengthened. Using larger or longer beads in your design will quickly achieve that purpose.

For variety, try using three different beads instead of three identical ones (as in the finished sample). Be sure to use beads that look good together, perhaps of a similar shape but different colors, or the same color but in different shapes.

Stacked Washer-Link
BRACELET

Simple, sophisticated links of textured copper washers form the basis for this ethnic-style bracelet design. It's easy to make in just a couple of hours with texturing hammers and good-quality pliers. Make sure to use heavy-duty flush cutters that are suitable for 12-gauge wire; alternatively, you could use 14-gauge or even 16-gauge wire to make the figure-eight links for your first attempt. *Tip:* If you can't find copper washers locally, yellow brass washers from a hardware store may be substituted.

materials

- Copper washers
- Round dead-soft 12-gauge wire (copper or silver), about 4' (122 cm)

tools

- Ruler
- Chasing hammer
- Small steel bench block
- Heavy-duty flush cutters
- Small embossing hammer
- 0000 (superfine) steel wool
- Jewelry pliers: small round-nose, chain-nose, flat-nose, and bail-forming

1 Thoroughly clean all of your wire with 0000 (superfine) steel wool. Flush-cut one end of the wire with flush cutters suitable for cutting up to 12-gauge wire.

2 Measure and flush-cut 2¼" (5.5 cm) of wire. Repeat until you have fifteen wire pieces measuring 2¼" (5.5 cm) each.

3 Place one wire in the large bail-forming pliers, with the smallest (6.8 mm) jaw facing away from you.

4 Roll the tool over in your hand until the wire end touches itself. Note that the wire is wrapped around the smaller jaw on the tool.

5 Repeat Steps 3–4 with the straight wire end until you have formed a large figure-eight link. Make sure that both wire ends touch. Repeat these steps with the remaining fourteen wire pieces from Step 2, until you have fifteen figure-eight links. Set them aside.

6 You will need a nice collection of copper washers to work with. I purchase mine in a kit from Harbor Freight (see the Resources section, p. 158), which provides a plastic box with dividers holding copper washers in five different sizes.

7 Select several washers in two different sizes. For the bracelet shown in the sample, I used seven large washers and six medium-size washers. Feel free to experiment by using washers in different sizes.

8 One at a time, texture one side of the copper washers using the larger end of a small embossing hammer. This will take some time.

9 *Option:* On the larger washers, which will later be stacked beneath the medium-size washers, texture just the outer edge with the smaller end of the small embossing hammer. This gives a three-dimensional appearance to your texturing.

10 Here's how the two washers look once they've been textured and stacked with the smaller washer on top of the larger one.

wire art jewelry workshop

11 Pick up a figure-eight link and open it sideways. Attach it to one stacked pair of washers and close the link sideways. Open the other side of the link and prepare to attach it to another pair of stacked washers.

12 Attach a second figure-eight link to two stacked-washer pairs. This step is not necessary, but the bracelet looks better when linked with doubled figure-eight links.

13 Here's how the pattern looks.

14 Attach the fifteenth figure-eight link to one end of the bracelet. Set it aside.

15 Flush-cut a 4" (10 cm) piece of 12-gauge wire and hammer each end with a chasing hammer. Spiral in the ends just a few times, each spiral facing the opposite direction. Grasp the wire in the middle near the back of the small round-nose pliers.

16 Bend a loop in the center of the wire around the round-nose pliers.

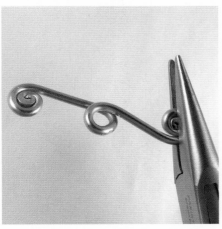

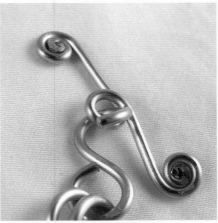

17 If necessary, spiral in each end just a bit more. You don't want a toggle that is too long to fit through a copper washer.

18 Attach the bar end of the toggle to the figure-eight link from Step 14. Close the figure-eight link sideways.

19 Here's how the finished bracelet looks, linked together, before it's been artificially aged in liver of sulfur (see the Basic Techniques section, p. 18). Note that the bar end of the toggle fits through a large copper washer that has not been stacked with a smaller washer.

stacked washer-link bracelet

Thai Heart
PENDANT

This is an easy way to turn a bead into a fancy pendant with a handmade spiral head pin and a double-wrapped eye-pin loop. Artificially aging the finished pendant in liver of sulfur and placing it on an interesting chain turns a simple project into an eye-catching neckpiece.

materials

- Necklace chain
- Heart-shaped bead
- Round dead-soft wire: 9"–12" (23–30.5 cm) of 14-gauge or 16-gauge and 12" (30.5 cm) 22-gauge

tools

- Flush cutters
- Chasing hammer
- Ruler, tape measure
- Small steel bench block
- 0000 (superfine) steel wool
- Jewelry pliers: small round-nose, chain-nose, and flat-nose

1 Start by choosing a heart-shaped bead, which can be made of glass, ceramic, metal, wood, or any other material. Look for a bead at least 1" (2.5 cm) long with a lengthwise hole large enough to accommodate 16-gauge or 14-gauge wire.

2 Test various gauges of wire on your bead until you've found the heaviest that will pass through the bead hole. In the sample shown, 14-gauge round dead-soft copper wire will be used.

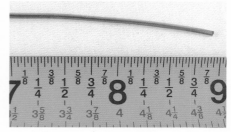

3 Clean all of your wire with 0000 (superfine) steel wool and then flush-cut the end of the heavy-gauge wire you'll be using to make the pendant. Flush-cut about 9" (23 cm) of this wire; note that you could use more wire for a larger bead, up to 12" (30.5 cm).

4 Hammer the wire end with a chasing hammer on a steel bench block. Then use the tips of the small round-nose pliers to form a tiny loop on this end of the wire. Switch to chain-nose or flat-nose pliers and continue spiraling the wire until it's between ¼" (6 mm) and ½" (1.3 cm) in diameter.

5 Place the heart bead on your work surface and place the spiral beneath it to determine if the spiral is big enough or if you need to spiral the wire a bit more. The size spiral you make for your heart bead is a personal choice.

6 Grasp the wire just above the spiral as shown, in the flat-nose pliers.

7 Bend the wire firmly against the spiral. It now resembles a lollipop and is ready to be used as a head pin for the heart-shaped bead.

8 *Option:* Hammer just the outer edges of the spiral using a chasing hammer on a steel bench block.

9 Place the bead on the wire.

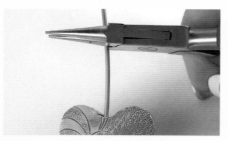

10 Grasp the wire about 1" (2.5 cm) above the bead in the back of the small round-nose pliers.

11 Bend the wire around to the right as shown.

12 Continue bending the wire around the bottom jaw of the pliers until you have one complete rotation, with the wire lying flat across the tool.

13 Switch to chain-nose pliers and bend the wire back sharply against the edge of the tool. This is known as "breaking the neck."

14 Remove the chain-nose pliers. Reinsert the round-nose pliers and place the tool in your left hand, with the bead facing away from you and the wrapping wire to the left.

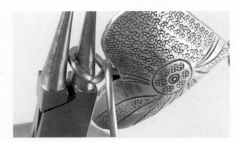

15 Use chain-nose pliers to wrap the wire over to the right.

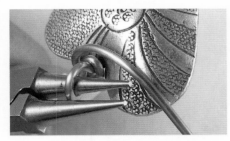

16 Wrap the wire under to the left and then over to the right again. This is known as "wrapping the neck."

17 Wrap the neck as many times as you prefer and then spiral in the remaining wire end. Tuck the spiral firmly against the bead. Note that in the sample I deliberately formed a loose, open spiral. Your own spiral can be large or small, loose or tight—it's a personal choice.

18 Here is the finished pendant, ready to be strung on a leather cord, some ribbon, a fancy chain, ball-chain, or a neck wire, (your choice).

19 *Option:* Begin wrapping the eye-pin loop made in Steps 11–18 with about 1' (30.5 cm) of 22-gauge wire (silver or copper, your choice). Bend the 22-gauge wire in half and place it on the eye-pin loop.

20 Wrap the 22-gauge wire around the 14-gauge wire very tightly, with coils lying adjacent to one another. Continue coiling.

21 Wrap the 22-gauge wire around the 14-gauge wire until you have completely covered the eye-pin loop.

22 Bring both wires to the back of the heart pendant and cross them.

23 After wrapping the wires in a tight loop near the base of the eye-pin loop, trim the wire ends with about 1½" (1.3 cm) remaining.

24 Spiral in the wire ends. Once both wire ends have been spiraled in, tuck them firmly against the bead with flat-nose pliers.

thai heart pendant

Grateful Heart
NECKLACE

By the time you finish this necklace, you will have mastered several techniques demonstrated in the Basic Techniques section—including doubled jump-ring sets, Celtic knot links, free-form knotless netting, coil-wrapped bead connectors, a handmade clasp, and more. The Grateful Heart pendant is a bold statement in 10-gauge wire, and the accompanying necklace features many beautiful and unusual wire links and bead wraps. If you prefer a simpler necklace design, just connect a commercial chain with clasp to each eye-pin loop wrapped on the outer edges of the Grateful Heart pendant.

materials

- Hook-and-eye clasp
- 4 Celtic knot links
- 4 coil-wrapped bead connectors
- 2 free-form knotless-netting embellished beads
- Round dead-soft wire: 5' (152.5 cm) 14-gauge, 1' (30.5 cm) 10-gauge
- About 9 bead dangles on commercial and/or handmade head pins

tools

- Flush cutters
- Hard-plastic mallet
- Ruler, tape measure
- 0000 (superfine) steel wool
- 4" x 4" (10 x 10 cm) square steel bench block
- Chasing hammer with a convex face
- Jewelry pliers: small round-nose, large round-nose, bail-forming, chain-nose, bent chain-nose, and flat-nose

1 Clean all of your wire thoroughly with 0000 (superfine) steel wool.

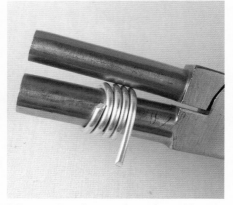

2 Prepare to make some jump rings with about 3' (91.5 cm) of round dead-soft 14-gauge wire. Form the jump rings on the larger (8.8 mm) jaw of the bail-forming pliers.

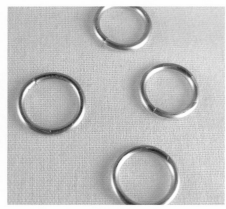

3 Make twenty-four jump rings; condition them and close each one as described in the Basic Techniques section.

4 Open one jump ring and insert it into another closed jump ring.

5 Close the second jump ring and set it aside. Repeat these steps until you have twelve doubled jump-ring sets (or more, for a longer necklace). Set them aside.

6 Make four coil-wrapped bead connectors as described in the Basic Techniques section. Set them aside.

7 Make a few sets of bead dangles on head pins as described in the Basic Techniques section. Set them aside.

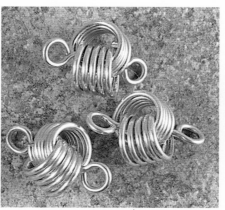

8 Make four to six Celtic knot links as described in the Basic Techniques section and set them aside.

9 Option: Make two free-form knotless-netting embellished beads as described in the Basic Techniques section. Set them aside.

wire art jewelry workshop

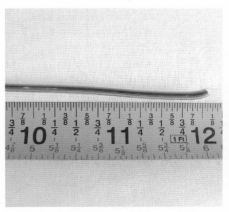

10 Flush-cut 1' (30.5 cm) of 10-gauge wire.

11 Using flat-nose pliers, bend the 10-gauge wire in half.

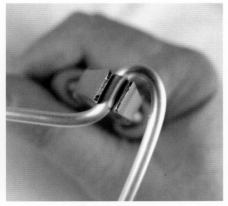

12 Using flat-nose pliers, bend the wire to the side, against the edge of the pliers.

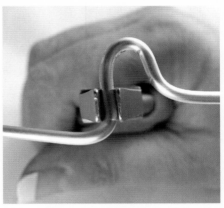

13 Repeat Step 12, bending the opposite wire end away from the first one. This is the tip of the heart.

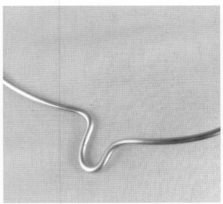

14 Use your fingertips to shape the wire ends in nice swooping curves away from the tip of the heart.

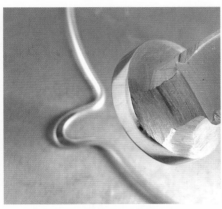

15 Using a chasing hammer and a 4" x 4" (10 x 10 cm) square steel bench block, hammer the tip of the heart. Don't overdo this step; the objective is to flatten the wire a bit, but not to thin it down too much.

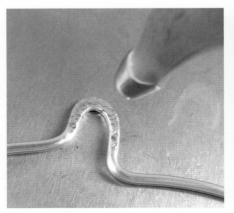

16 Use a small embossing hammer to texture the tip of the heart.

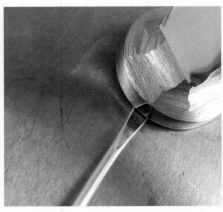

17 Use a chasing hammer and bench block to forge one end of the heart-shaped wire.

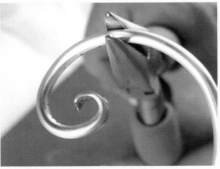

18 Bend a small loop in this wire end near the tips of the large round-nose pliers. The loop should face toward the center of the heart. Switch to chain-nose pliers and bend a large, loose spiral in the wire end, spiraling toward the center of the heart.

grateful heart necklace

19 Place three bead dangles on the heart, running the straight wire end of the heart-shaped wire through each eye-pin loop on each bead dangle. Allow the bead dangles to slide down the wire until they stop at the tip of the heart.

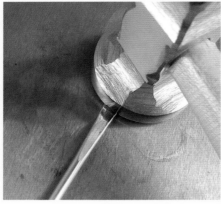

20 Use a chasing hammer and bench block to forge the remaining wire end of the heart-shaped wire.

21 Repeat Step 18 to shape the top section of the heart.

22 Use a hard-plastic mallet to hammer the top half of the heart.

23 Switch to a chasing hammer and, placing the top portion of the heart-shaped wire on a 4" x 4" (10 x 10 cm) size steel bench block, hammer just the outer edges of the heart. Switch to a small embossing hammer and use it to texture the flattened areas of the heart-shaped wire.

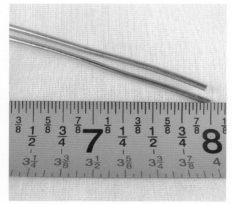

24 Measure and flush-cut two 8" (20.5 cm) lengths of 14-gauge wire.

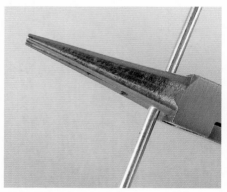

25 Take up one 8" (20.5 cm) wire length in the back of the small round-nose pliers, grasping the wire in the middle.

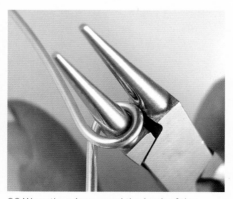

26 Wrap the wire around the back of the pliers, forming a loop.

27 Open the loop sideways and place two to three bead dangles on it. Close the loop sideways securely.

wire art jewelry workshop

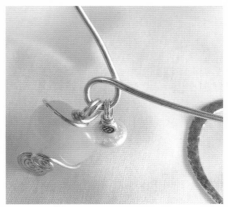

28 Repeat Steps 25–27 with the second 14-gauge wire piece, adding a couple bead dangles to the loop.

29 Place one of the 14-gauge wire pieces against the outer edge of the heart-shaped wire piece to determine its placement.

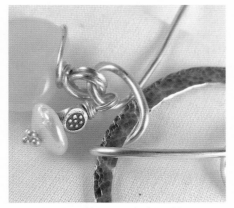

30 Begin wrapping one end of the 14-gauge wire around the outer edge of the heart-shaped wire piece.

31 Continue wrapping the wire, but reserve a 1" (2.5 cm) tail to turn into a spiral later.

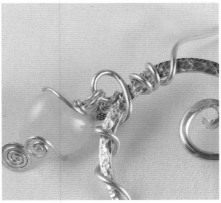

32 Wrap the other end of the 14-gauge wire as in Steps 30–31, again reserving some straight wire to turn into a spiral.

33 Hammer the wire ends with a chasing hammer.

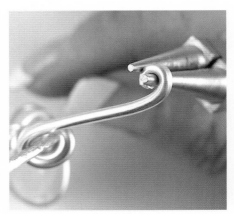

34 Spiral in one wire end by starting a tiny loop in the wire on the tips of the small round-nose pliers.

35 Switch to chain-nose pliers and spiral in the wire until it meets the heart-shaped wire piece.

36 Use the tips of the tool to press the spiral firmly against the heart-shaped wire piece.

grateful heart necklace

37 Repeat Steps 34–36 with the second wire end. Any tool marks can be filed away later with a jeweler's file.

38 Repeat all of these Steps (25–37) with the second 14-gauge wire piece. Here you can see the finished Grateful Heart pendant.

39 Attach one of the large doubled jump-ring sets made in Steps 2–5 to one of the eye-pin loops on the outer edge of the Grateful Heart pendant.

40 Close the jump rings securely.

41 To these jump rings, attach a coil-wrapped bead connector, opening and closing its eye-pin loop sideways.

42 Repeat Steps 39–41 on the opposite side of the Grateful Heart pendant.

43 Open the eye-pin loop on a Celtic knot link sideways.

44 Attach a large doubled jump-ring set.

45 Attach the other end of the doubled jump-ring set to the coil-wrapped bead connector.

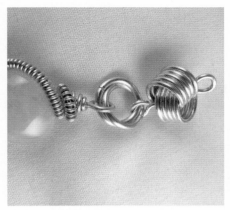

46 Here is how the pattern should look.

47 Open the second eye-pin loop on the Celtic knot link sideways.

48 Attach a large doubled jump-ring set.

49 Open both jump rings and attach them to a free-form knotless netting bead connector. Continue the necklace pattern by adding: a doubled jump-ring set, a coil-wrapped bead connector, a doubled jump-ring set, and a Celtic knot link (see p. 31).

50 Attach the "eye" of a hook-and-eye clasp to one end of the necklace. Note: The hook-and-eye clasp is demonstrated in the Basic Techniques section.

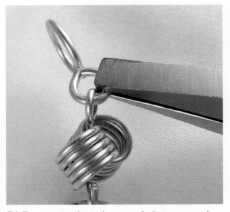

51 Be sure to close the eye-pin loop securely.

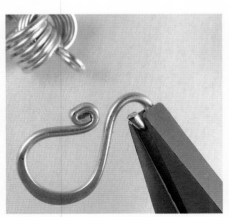

52 Repeat Steps 39–51 with the opposite side of the necklace. End by attaching the "hook" portion of the hook-and-eye clasp.

53 Be sure to close the eye-pin loop securely.

grateful heart necklace

Wrap-A-Rock
PENDANT

There's more than one way to wrap a rock to make a pendant for a piece of jewelry. I myself have several ways of doing this, and I'm sure there are other artists with many different ideas of their own. But this is one of my favorites; it's a little unusual with no less than four wrapped eye-pin loops, opening up more creative possibilities for suspending the pendant.

I found this rock while teaching a workshop on the island of Santorini in 2008. Although it's fairly large at 2" x 2½" (5 x 6.5 cm), it's lightweight. That's the type of rock to look for when choosing a pendant stone.

materials

- Round dead-soft 18-gauge wire, about 54" (137 cm)
- Necklace chain of some type (rubber cording, ball-chain, etc.)

tools

- Flush cutters
- Tape measure
- Medium-size stone
- 0000 (superfine) steel wool
- Jewelry pliers: small round-nose, chain-nose, and flat-nose

1 Clean your wire thoroughly with 0000 (superfine) steel wool or with polishing pads.

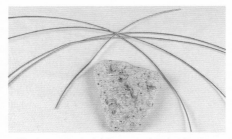

2 Flush-cut several 18-gauge dead-soft wire pieces. For the rock shown here, I cut four 12" (30.5 cm) long pieces plus one 6" (15 cm) piece to wrap them together. If you use a larger or smaller rock, you'll have to estimate how much wire is needed to wrap it. *Tip:* You always need more wire than you think you will need.

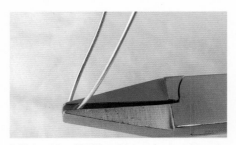

3 Pick up the 6" (15 cm) wire piece and bend it in half in the flat-nose pliers.

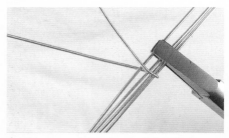

4 Hold the remaining four wire pieces together side by side and wrap the 6" (15 cm) piece around them.

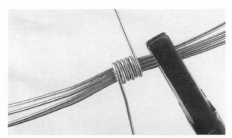

5 As you wrap the bundle of wires, keep them flat, side by side, by pressing them firmly with flat-nose pliers.

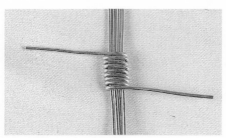

6 Stop wrapping when you have about ¾" (2 cm) of straight wire protruding out from both sides of the wire bundle. Both wires must be on the same side of the bundle as shown.

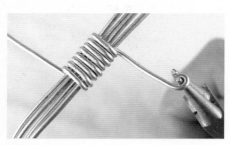

7 Begin a small spiral in the tips of the small round-nose pliers.

8 Use flat-nose pliers to squeeze the beginning spiral tightly.

9 Continue spiraling the wire until it lays down nicely on the bundle. Repeat these steps with the other straight wire piece.

10 Gently bend the wire ends up using flat-nose pliers.

11 Check the bend against the bottom of the rock you're about to wrap. It should conform very closely to the rock's shape.

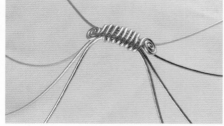

12 Spread out the wire "spokes"; note that there are four on each side. Here's how it looks from the underside.

wire art jewelry workshop

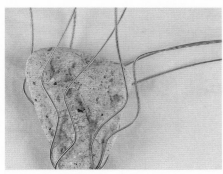

13 Bend the wires up around the rock, four on the front and four on the back. Begin shaping the wire gently with your fingers to create undulating waves. You can also use your tools to shape the wires.

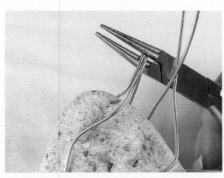

14 Start making eye-pin loops on the top of the pendant. Grasp one wire from the front of the rock and one from the back and wrap them together in the small round-nose pliers.

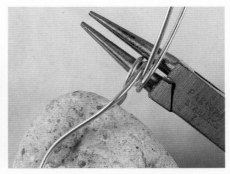

15 Wrap all the way around, one complete rotation. You will only need to wrap the wire once around, but because you're using two wires together, the end result will appear to be a double-wrapped eye-pin loop.

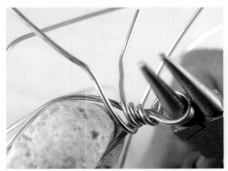

16 Wrap the "neck" area between the loop and the top of the rock. Pull the wires around tightly with chain-nose pliers.

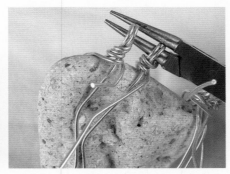

17 Repeat these steps until you've made four wrapped eye-pin loops at the top of the pendant.

18 Time to take care of those pesky wire ends! You could trim them with flush cutters, but I like to spiral them in. Use small round-nose pliers to start each spiral.

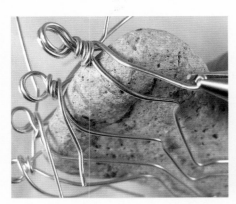

19 Squeeze it tightly with chain-nose pliers.

20 Continue the spiral and tuck it against the top of the rock, or anywhere else you'd like to see the spiral.

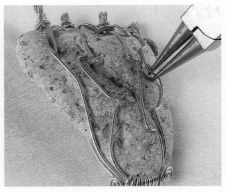

21 Use round-nose pliers to grasp each wire and give it a twist or two. This adds a beautiful decorative element to the design and also tightens the wires around the rock, holding it firmly in place. ***Tip:*** Don't use chain-nose pliers for this step because they have a tendency to cut the wire.

Dancing Man
NECKLACE

materials

- 6 worm beads
- Hook-and-eye clasp
- 11 large bead connectors
- 1 pendant bead of any size or shape
- Round dead-soft wire: 6" (15 cm) 14-gauge
- 15 large jump rings in 14-gauge or 12-gauge wire
- About 70 small bead dangles on head pins with wrapped eye-pin loops

tools

- Flush cutters
- Ruler, tape measure
- Small steel bench block
- 0000 (superfine) steel wool
- Chasing hammer with a convex face
- Jewelry pliers: small round-nose, chain-nose, flat-nose, and bail-forming

Sometimes you purchase a special pendant bead, then wait years to design just the right jewelry piece around it. That was the case with my turquoise carved "dancing man" pendant, purchased at least a decade ago in a bead shop on the beach. The shop has closed since then, but I still have fond memories of spending an afternoon picking out just a few pricey items that I couldn't live without. Recently I discovered a way to match my pendant with Peruvian opal beads, Thai-silver shells, and handmade worm beads. I hope you enjoy making something similar with one of your treasured beads.

1 Assemble your materials first. You'll need eleven large beads on wrapped eye-pin links (see the Basic Techniques section) plus one pendant bead of some type, any size or shape. The pendant bead might need a jump ring to connect it to the necklace.

2 You'll also need six worm beads (see the Basic Techniques section) of various sizes.

3 Assemble about seventy small bead dangles on commercial or handmade head pins. You can use the beads, crystals, pearls, silver spacer beads, etc., of your choice.

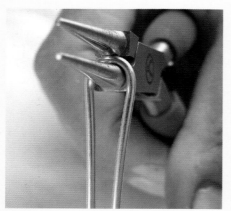

4 The first step is to connect the pendant bead to one of the large bead connectors using a large jump ring.

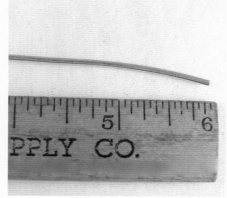

5 To make the connection, first flush-cut 6" (15 cm) of 14-gauge round dead-soft wire.

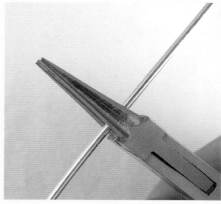

6 Grasp the middle of the wire in the back of the small round-nose pliers.

7 Keeping the pliers still, use your fingers to bend the wire around the back of the tool. Make sure to keep the wire ends even.

8 Wrap the wire one complete rotation around the tool.

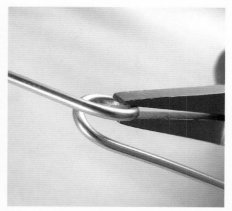

9 Remove the round-nose pliers and open the loop sideways with flat-nose pliers.

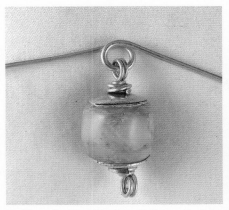

10 Place the large bead connector on the loop and close the loop sideways.

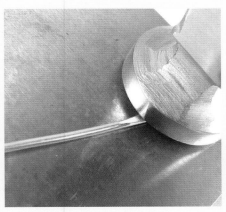

11 Hammer flat the two wire ends.

12 Begin spiraling in the wire ends in the tips of the small round-nose pliers.

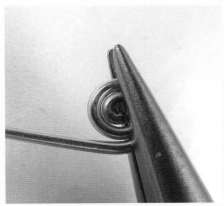

13 Switch to chain-nose pliers and spiral in the wire toward the center.

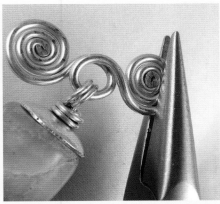

14 Stop spiraling in the wire ends when they meet the center loop.

15 Open the jump ring on the pendant and attach it to the double-spiral link you just made.

16 Here's how your necklace looks so far.

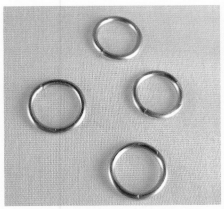

17 Make fifteen large jump rings using either 12-gauge (shown) or 14-gauge round dead-soft wire. Condition them and close them before proceeding.

18 Open one jump ring and run it through the double-wrapped eye-pin loop on the large bead connector from Step 16.

dancing man necklace

19 Place five small bead dangles on one side of the jump ring.

20 Place a worm bead on the jump ring. Then place five more small bead dangles and a worm bead on the other side of the large bead dangle. Prepare to close the jump ring sideways.

21 Here is how the necklace looks with two worm beads holding a jump ring loaded with ten small bead dangles and the large bead connector with pendant.

22 Open another jump ring and attach it to one of the worm beads. Add five small bead dangles and another large bead connector to the jump ring.

23 When you close the jump ring, this is how the pattern looks. Observe that the bead dangles are placed on one side of the jump ring so that when the necklace is worn, they'll hang correctly.

24 Open another jump ring and attach it to the large bead connector from the previous step. Add five small bead dangles and another large bead connector to the jump ring.

25 When you close the jump ring, this is how the pattern looks.

wire art jewelry workshop

26 Continue adding large bead connectors and worm beads to both sides of the necklace, each jump ring holding five small bead dangles. *Tip:* Near the back of the necklace, you may cease adding bead dangles if there is concern about them getting tangled in your hair. When the necklace has reached the desired length, add a hook-and-eye clasp.

27 Here is the "eye" of the hook-and-eye clasp. I suggest making the clasp for this necklace with a heavy-gauge wire such as 14-gauge. See the Basic Techniques section (p. 18) for instruction on making this type of clasp. Attach the hook to the opposite necklace end.

28 Close the loop firmly to create a secure clasp.

dancing man necklace

This is one of my very favorite necklace designs, but I won't kid you: It was very expensive to make! If you haven't guessed it already, I used a ton of sterling silver wire to make all of its components, jump rings, and bead dangles. I did not stint on using fine-silver shell beads, pricey Peruvian opal, pearls, commercial head pins, and a costly carved turquoise pendant.

It's a showstopper, one of a kind. Every jewelry artist should have at least one very special piece to wear and treasure always. But I also understand that with silver prices going up every day, this necklace is expensive to duplicate.

I have a few solutions to this dilemma:

• Make your necklace using either copper wire or a mix of some copper and some sterling silver wire.

• Make the necklace shorter.

• Make it with fewer bead dangles.

• Substitute inexpensive wooden beads for the pricey fine-silver shells and Peruvian opals I used.

• Use fewer worm beads to reduce your wire usage, substituting other wire links demonstrated throughout this book.

Most of all, have fun with your necklace. Alter it as you please, adding and subtracting elements as your budget and sense of design dictate. Trust your own creative intuition to guide you and soon you'll have a special, one-of-a-kind necklace that's not for sale, not for any price!

Asia Charisma

asia-charisma.net

asiacharisma@gmail.com

Fine-silver beads, bead caps, clasps, and jewelry findings from the Karen hill tribes of Thailand

Bass Pro Shops

basspro.com

(800) 227-7776

Fishing tackle boxes ideal for storing and organizing beads and jewelry components

Harbor Freight

harborfreight.com

(805) 388-3000

Copper washers, inexpensive tools, drills, metal hole-punches, files, steel wool

Rio Grande

riogrande.com

(800) 545-6566

Quality tools for jewelry making, hammers, bench blocks, files, Fretz embossing hammers, center punch, metal bracelet mandrels, liver of sulfur, wire, sheet metal

Shipwreck Beads

shipwreckbeads.com

(800) 950-4232

Vast assortment of beads and pearls, including small metal beads with large holes

Thunderbird Supply

thunderbirdsupply.com

(505) 722-4323

Quality tools for jewelry making, wire, sheet metal, liver of sulfur, metal beads and charms, hard-plastic and rawhide mallets, hammers

Tronex Tools

tronextools.com

(707) 426-2550

Specialty flush cutters and pliers

Wired Up Beads

wiredupbeads.com

(817) 937-8500

Pliers, flush cutters, beads, jewelry making

wire art jewelry workshop

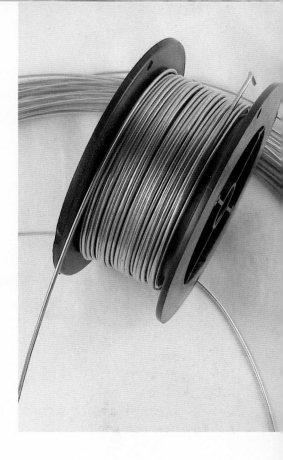

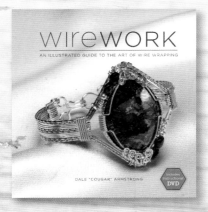